COMPOUND YELLOW MANUAL

of
Prompts, Provocations, Permissions,
& Parameters for Everyday Practices

Edited
by
JORGE LUCERO
&
LAURA SHAEFFER

Published on the occasion of our participation
in *Artist Run Chicago 2.0*
The Hyde Park Art Center, Chicago, IL
APRIL 6 - JUNE 12, 2020

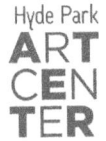 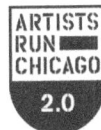 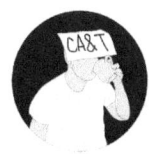

COMPOUND YELLOW IS AN INDEPENDENT, EXPERIMENTAL
ARTS SPACE IN OAK PARK, IL.

We are a non-profit 501(c)(3) experimental art space with a
curatorial focus in cultural production, sharing economies,
participatory art, and interdisciplinary explorations.
Comprised of a group of artists, curators, educators, parents
and engaged citizens, Compound Yellow hosts exhibitions,
interventions, performances, workshops, lectures, gatherings,
and collective imagining. We want to celebrate a culture of
sharing, connecting and collective action! We'd love to hear
from you.

Compound Yellow is run by Laura Shaeffer, Founding
Director.

We continue to work with a long list of collaborators
including Lora Lode (co-founder of CY), Anna Ogier-
Bloomer, Hannah Barco, Alberto Aguilar, Atlan Arceo-Wiltz,
Maggie Leininger, Regin Igloria, Jeff Levrant, Matthew
Nicholas (a co-founder of CY), Andrew Nord, Jasper Nord,
Tony Foley, Erik Peterson, Melissa Potter, Alisa Reith,
Michael Greene, Jorge Lucero, Gabriel Soto, and Ryan
Thompson. And we are grateful for the ongoing support of
our many interns and volunteers!

Compound Yellow accepts unsolicited proposals for art and
design projects and exhibitions, workshops and educational
programming, community activities, and more. To submit a
proposal visit https://compoundyellow.com/submit-a-proposal.

www.compoundyellow.com
www.hydeparkart.org
www.jorgelucero.com/conceptual-art-and-teaching

Contributors to this publication

Collaborators, affiliates, and stakeholders
with Compound Yellow worldwide

Alberto Aguilar, Madeleine Aguilar, Katrin Asbury, Hannah
Barco, Erik Bartholomew, Kayce Bayer, Rebecca Beachy, Marrisa
Lee Benedict, Robert Beshara, Brett Bloom, David Boykin, Kat
Bunke, Jessica Charlesworth, Andi L. Christ, Jeremy Cohan, Kate
Conlon, William Cordova, Angel Bat Dawid, Alex DeGraaf,
Katherine Desjardins, Tiny Domingos, Christa Donner, Jim
Duignan, Amanda Englert, William Estrada, Marianne
Fairbanks, Frances Figg, Marc Fischer, Tony Foley, Conrad
Freiburg, Matthew Giddings, Alex Gilliam, Mejay Gula, Judith
Heineman, Desiree Heiss, Erica Hess, Kiku hibino, Sam Hill,
Amanda Hirkshorn, Hirvitalo, Brian Holmes, Boyang Hou, Drea
Howenstein, Spencer Hutchinson, Regin Igloria, Ion N55, Luke
Joyner, Ines Kaag, Mark Klein, Wilfried Kuehn, Maggie
Leininger, Chris Lin, Lora Lode, Norman Long, Jorge Lucero,
Gwenn-ael Lynn, April Lynn & Adam Rose, Faheem Majeed,
Jesse Malmed, Curtis Meyer, Hani Moustafa, Justin Nalley,
Matthew Nicholas, ANDERS Nilsen, Andrew Nord, Jasper Nord,
Sebastian Nord, Michelle Nordmeyer, Anna Ogier-Bloomer,
Julian Otis, Teresa Pankratz, Tim Parsons, Lorenza Perreli, Dan
Peterman, Andrew Gryf Paterson, Mike Phillips, Mel Potter,
Marne Provost, Maggie Queeney, Allison Peters Quinn, Kevin
Reiswig, Alisa Reith, Casey Roberts, Amina Ross, Nathaniel
Russell, Christopher Santiago, David Schalliol, Matthew Serlo,
Doug Shaeffer, Ben Shepard, Plus Sign, Hoyun Son, Edra Soto,
Gabriel Soto, Albert Stabler, Vanessa Stokes, Lizzy Swaya, Nel
Taylor, Norman Teague, Rachel Tredon, Hui-Min Tsen, Serge
Vutuc, Rachel Wallis, Aaron Walker, Sean Ward, Tessa Windt,
Sadie Woods, Natalie Wright, Mary Zerkel, Ji Yang Zhu, and
Rebecca Zorach

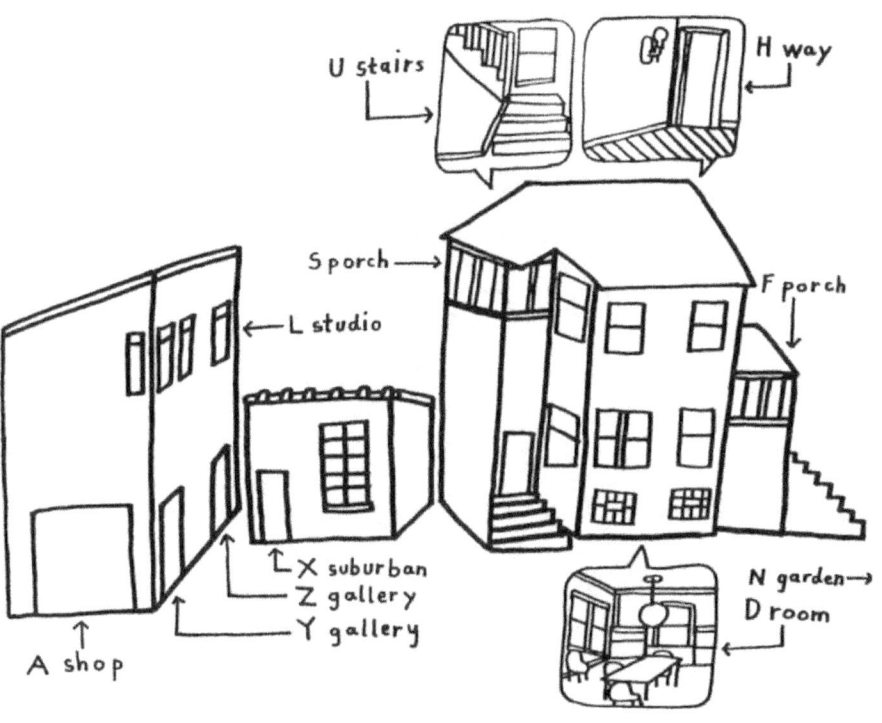

U stairs

H way

S porch

F porch

L studio

X suburban
Z gallery
Y gallery

A shop

N garden
D room

Diagram of CY by Madeleine Aguilar

5

Introduction
Jorge Lucero

Compound Yellow is a Hub of Production

In 2013 *The Atlantic* assembled a panel of prominent scientist, entrepreneurs, and inventors to compile a comprehensive list of 50 of the most essential human inventions. The panel of scholars was asked to only include things created after the advent of the wheel, 6,000 years ago. The disparate list, which includes everything from alphabetization and paper to vaccinations and the Internet is striking— not because of how the globe has obviously been redefined by these human achievements—rather because of how invisible most of these creations have become over time. Not unlike the wheel, the majority of the world's greatest inventions have receded into the unnoticeable hum of ubiquity, and that is—in fact—part of what classifies these creations as vital. When things like electricity, the Gregorian Calendar, cement, and the common nail do their "thing" under the surface of the human experience they demonstrate themselves to be the life-giving gears –or wheels, if you will—that make the whole enterprise run.

Compound Yellow, an art and community space born and operated from Laura Shaefer's family home in Oak Park, Illinois is the hub of an infinitely churning wheel that actively propels Chicago's continued place as the epicenter of a certain kind of *pedagogy-as-art-practice,* which dates back to Jane

Addams' Hull House and John Dewey's Lab School. The history of Chicago's activity in this realm courses through the spectacle-activism of Saul Alinsky all the way to the embedded community work of the Stockyard Institute. These and hundreds of other examples are momentarily documented in part by Mary Jane Jacob and Kate Zeller's five-volume *Chicago Social Practice History Series* (2014-15). I refer to this pedagogy-as-art-practice occurring in a realm, rather than a form, because of its innate—almost inevitable—amorphousness. This realm only sometimes reveals itself as art; it only occasionally looks like some *thing*. Most of the time this realm (and those who practice in it) just emanate, radiating like spokes from a hub; like compounded rays from a bright yellow sun. Compound Yellow is predominately a work of affect; not because it isn't consistently manifesting itself through the events, objects, and visuals of socially engaged art (e.g. participatory exhibitions, collaborative learning, community organizing, horizontalized generativity, books, prints, performances, photographs, and websites), rather because what it really does is so immense that it is difficult to document, show, or even talk about in any way that is truly representative.

As such, the only real way to describe Compound Yellow or show the evidence of what it *does* is by looking at its radiating spokes individually or in compilations. This book is an incomplete and imperfect compilation of some of those individual spokes (aka friends of CY). It's obviously "incomplete" because everyone who has ever come in contact with or collaborated with Compound Yellow is not included in this book (see affiliates and collaborators on page 4 of this book); and I say "imperfect" because what you will find in this book is not whole spokes emanating from the hub that is Compound Yellow, rather slivers from those who were able to contribute at the moment we were assembling this book.

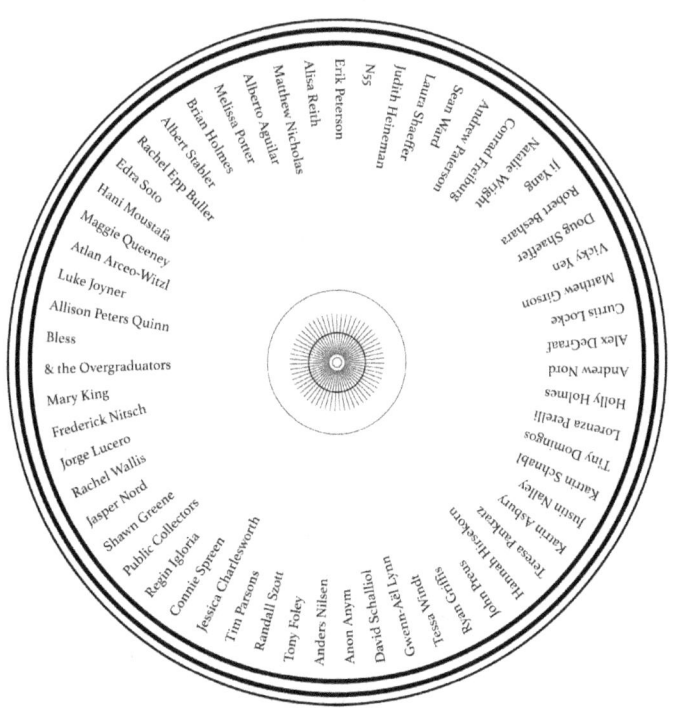

Each contributor has taken a sliver from their practice—a practice that at some point has been in contact with Compound Yellow—and donated it to this book as either a prompt, provocation, permission or parameter. What are they for? They serve two purposes: 1. To catalog a fleeting moment in the work being done in and around Compound Yellow and 2. To offer opportunities for further making and thinking in relation to something made or thought up by a Compound Yellow friend. Each entry offers the reader a filter by which they can examine the world anew and suggestions by which they might enact a behavior—artistic or otherwise—in the world.

This book has been composed on the occasion of Compound Yellow being invited to participate in the Hyde Park Art Center's *Artist-Run Chicago 2.0*, an exhibition that features fifty manifestations of the same shared, resourceful ethos which I'm referring to a few paragraphs back. It is an urgency to live as a civically engaged artistic community at various levels in both moments of plenitude and times of crisis. It just so happens that as we were assembling this book, the world fell into just that. All of the authors in this book sent their contributions through email, noting how glad they were to have had this assignment in the midst of the Covid-19 pandemic. Counterintuitively to one of the pillars of Compound Yellow's mission, everyone had to keep their physical distance, but this project gave us the much-needed opportunity to still come together.

Compound Yellow is difficult to describe; it is however, not difficult to be a part of. Laura Shaeffer has been the hub of production known as Op Shop, SHoP, and now Compound Yellow for twenty years and most of the work that she has facilitated will never be articulated in any fair manner that could make it either fully archivable or researchable; but that doesn't mean that it is not carried in the bodies and spirits of those who have come in contact with it. The work inevitably is invisible, but that doesn't make it any less present. You'll notice that many of the contributors to this book have included information about how they can be contacted. We reach out to each other through virtual means that are nevertheless very real. We feel it now more than ever and this is how the invisible wheel keeps turning; it's how the hub keeps radiating.

So, keep *in touch*.
-Jorge Lucero
www.jorgelucero.com

Alberto Aguilar

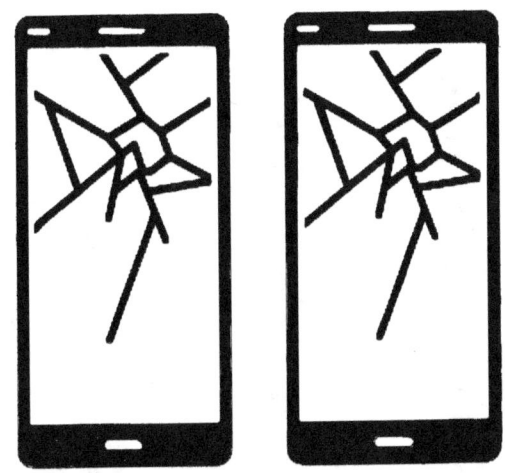

With my map at hand
I locate the repair shop
to fix my cracked glass.

this pole stands in mem-

this pole stands in
ory of

memory of this

here I mark this spot

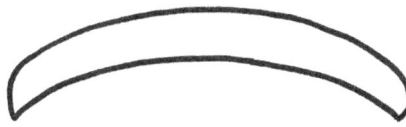

on the side of this here street

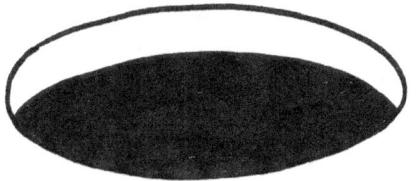

with this gaping hole

*3 Haiku Pictographs originally made for Western Pole,
but never shown, (2019). Pen on standard print paper.*

Anon Anym

"Jamie, we have half an hour now during this drive. What is the most important thing we can be thinking about?"

-R. Buckminster Fuller to his grandson Jamie Snyder, Operation Manual for Spaceship Earth

Atlan Arceo-Witzl

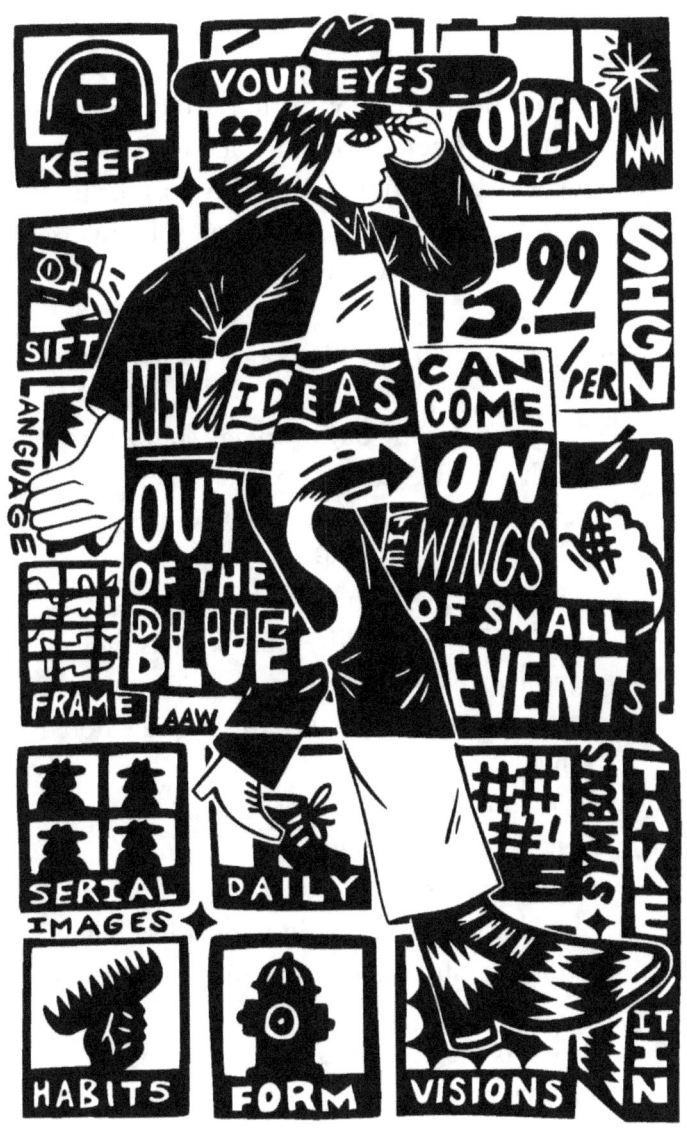

19

Take the time to note your rituals (routines/habits) throughout the course of a day or a week. Write down your observations, draw images, take photos/video, collect artifacts, and/or whatever you else you need to record your experience.

Some questions to consider when observing:

- What rituals in your everyday stand out?
- With what frequency do you perform these rituals? Yearly, monthly, weekly, everyday or multiple times a day?
- Are there objects involved in these practices? What are they and what is their significance?
- Where do these rituals happen and who is involved?
- Why do you repeat these rituals? What is their significance to you, to your culture, to our society?
- Are there gestures, actions, or steps that define the ritual? Are they done in a specific order?
- What is the usefulness of the actions in said ritual?
- How would you describe this ritual to someone who has never done it?

- When you imagine this ritual in practice, what images immediately come to mind? Are there symbols?

Take what you have gathered from your observations and compose a tribute to one ritual in particular. This might be a replication of an objected used, an illustration of the actions involved, an exaggerated or careful performance of your ritual, a model of your ritual space (miniature or life size), written directions of how to execute the ritual, etc. Think of your piece as a documentation of your experience and mindset. Taking the time to understand the mundane can provide an unexpected sense of grounding in what we value through our passing days.

Katrin Asbury

α cells:
GLUCAGON
acts on liver when blood glucose low

β cells:
INSULIN
acts on liver when blood glucose high

δ cells:
SOMATOSTATIN
inhibits glucagon & insulin

Glypizide (sulfonylurea) stimulates insulin production by functional β-cells left in pancreas

ISLES OF LANGERHANS

Diabetes

Mellitus:
Loss of insulin of decreased insulin responsiveness
(INSULIN DEPENDENT (dogs))
NON-INSULIN DEPENDENT

- POLYDIPSIA/POLYURIA
- POLYPHAGIA
- HYPERGLYCEMIA
- WEIGHT LOSS
- CATARACTS
- PLANTIGRADE POSTURE

Can cause ketoacidosis due to mobilization of fat

* Transitional is only in urinary system

* Pseudostratified is in trachea & bronchus

* Stratified cuboidal is in excretory or sweat & in salivary glands

Pseudostratified

Bronchus/trachea

ALL TOUCH BASAL LAMINA

Stratified

- skin esophagus vagina

BASAL LAYER IS <u>ACTIVE</u> MITOTIC

SIMPLE TUBULAR

SIMPLE BRANCHED TUBULAR

COMPOUND TUBULAR - Glands

SIMPLE ACINAR-Intestinal

MUCUS: Tubular SEROUS: acini

Submandibular Salivary gland

COMPOUND ACINAR OR ALVEOLAR- Submandibular Salivary gland

mucus secreting glands

mucus secreting glands

<u>Glands</u>

MEROCRINE: exocytosis of granules
APOCRINE: apical cytoplasm is released SWEAT
HOLOCRINE: whole cell is released SEBACEOUS SWEAT

Sweat Glands are the only SIMPLE COILED TUBULAR

CUBOIDAL STRATIFIED

SIMPLE CUBOIDAL

COMPOUND BRANCHED TUBULAR - Brunner's gland of Duodenum

SIMPLE BRANCHED ACINAR

SIMPLE ACINAR - Penile urethra (mucus)

sebaceous gland hair follicle

COMPOUND ACINAR

Robert Beshara

N.A.R.T.[1]
(The Network of Artists, Researchers, and Teachers)[2]
presents

The Nartist Manifesto

1. In the spirit of eclecticism, I choose to label myself a **Transdisciplinary Nartist** (occasionally abbreviated as **Trans-Nartist**) because the word **"artist"**[3] is too generic and the term **"fine artist"**[4] is hardly used.

2. I choose to be a non-artist because I reject the pretentiousness, materialism, and purposelessness of the art world today, which is chiefly postmodern—whatever that means! Instead I choose to embrace a more **meta/neo/re-modernist** approach.

---

[1] The Network of Art, Research, and Timelessness; The Nutopian Association of Research and Therapy; The Natural Artists' Revival of Truth; The Nonsensical Art of Recent Times; The Nonsense Alliance of Ridiculous Treaties; The Notorious Affiliation of Radical Titans; The Numerous Assholes Running Thebes; The Noetic Aphorism of Random Tautology; The National Academy of Rudimentary Tao.

[2] https://www.facebook.com/TransNartist

[3] Art (n.): "the conscious use of skill and creative imagination especially in the production of aesthetic objects; *also*: works so produced" (Merriam-Webster). Here's my variation on the former definition, but I attempt to define what an artist is and does. An artist is someone who consciously and unconsciously uses his or her skills and creative imagination [i.e. talent] in the creation of [tangible and/or intangible] aesthetic objects, environments, or experiences that can be shared with others, and which can appeal to the body, mind, and heart.

[4] Fine Art (n.): "art (as painting, sculpture, or music) concerned primarily with the creation of beautiful objects —usually used in plural" (Merriam-Webster). Then the question shifts from: what is art to what is **beauty**?

3. I am neither an artist nor a fartist, but I can typically be found between both categories.
4. By using the word "**Transdisciplinary**," I acknowledge the healthy paradox in things.
5. Nart is both spaceless and timeless. It is universal: always here and now. The present is the **only** reality that exists. But what is reality?
6. We perceive almost everything in this multi-dimensional reality called **Life** through our five senses. This perception is then filtered, through our brains. In essence, it's an electro-chemical process, no different from living in a virtual world.
7. Modern physics tells us that the Universe is roughly **70%** dark energy, **25%** of which is dark matter, and that **everything** we know as humans so far constitutes **5%** of this big picture[5]. We understand about **10%** of how our brains function[6]. On average **57%** of our total body weight is water[7]. Water (in the form of oceans) covers **71%** of the Earth's surface[8]. How are these statistics related?
8. The Nartist draws heavily from the **Collective Unconscious**[9] informing the **Collective**

---

[5] http://science.nasa.gov/astrophysics/focus-areas/what-is-dark-energy/
[6] http://www.scientificamerican.com/article.cfm?id=people-only-use-10-percent-of-brain
[7] Guyton, Arthur C. (1976). *Textbook of Medical Physiology* (5th ed.). Philadelphia: W.B. Saunders. p. 424
[8] http://www.noaa.gov/ocean.html
[9] "In Jungian psychology, a part of the unconscious mind, shared by a society, a people, or all humankind, that is the product of ancestral experience and contains such concepts as science, religion, and morality" (The Free Dictionary)

Consciousness; both comprise the *noosphere* or **Big Mind**, of which the Internet is a part.

9. The **disciplinary** is that which relates to discipline and practice. Practice relates to skill and discipline relates to persistence. Both result from hard work.

10. Nartistically, emphasis is given to performance-based art that is improvisational and/or interactive. Interests include the experimental and the avant-garde, the surreal and the absurd... the dada and de nada. The key is catharsis.

11. Having no purpose on purpose can be purposeful but not always. **Play** is key.

12. There is no fourth wall.

13. There is no frame.

14. There are no rules, only games.

15. Nart transcends science, but includes it all the same.

16. We are interested in the following scientific fields especially in how they relate to art and spirituality: mathematics (esp. sacred geometry), psychoanalysis, and physics (esp. quantum mechanics).

17. Science is incomplete like every other human discipline, but at least it is based on facts. However, facts are not truths, they are fragments: Particles of the Truth, so we also need the Waves of Light: those higher frequencies akin to the music of the spheres.

18. We, Nartists, want to be one with the Source[10], where we once came from... wherefrom this whole Universe originated: that single point.

19. First, there was the agricultural revolution then came the industrial revolution followed by the digital revolution. We are now entering a new epoch: the beginning of the emotional revolution—as is clear from the Arab Spring and the Occupy Together movement among others—, which will hopefully lead to our spiritual evolution.

20. God[11] created imperfect mortals, while human beings created perfect immortals through works of Nart as in sculpture.

21. Unlike Descartes: "I am therefore I am when I am wherever I happen to be."

22. We, at N.A.R.T., place an emphasis (in most Nartistic projects) on non-verbal communication through Sound, Color, and Movement because we realize that everything in this world (animate and inanimate) vibrates. The higher the frequency, the more healing it is. Besides, **55 to 70%** of our communication is non-verbal[12]. This methodology renders Nartistic projects pluriversal.

23. We aim to heal, inspire, educate, entertain, shock, and enlighten others and ourselves.

---

[10] Also known as God, Allah, the Great Spirit, Nature, etc.

[11] I am using the word "God" loosely here outside any religious context. I am of the opinion, however, that in order for a Creation to exist there must be a Creator (possibly as a complex system).

[12] http://www3.aaos.org/education/csmp/NonVerbalCommunication.cfm

24. We aim to transcend our egos by offering our service to help others hence uniting and strengthening the community in a positive way à la the Butterfly Effect.
25. We vow to be vegetarians and to grow our own produce.
26. We vow to meditate and to exercise daily.
27. We vow to be aware of our thoughts and actions as much as we can (aka mindfulness).
28. We speak from the heart and not the mind in order to purify the spirit.
29. We wish to unite with our twin flame (our significant other). We wish to befriend our soul mates lest we one day all return to our soul-cloud of origin and ultimately to the Source.
30. We acknowledge the existence of extraterrestrials, good and bad, here on Earth and beyond.
31. We are aware that achieving peace on Earth will be very hard (yet not impossible) because Gaia is on the first of nine planes and because we live in a world of contrasts (i.e., in order for peace to exist, there must be war, but war and peace can be within).
32. As Nartists, we do not live in a bubble. We are active human beings consciously taking part in this world in a myriad of ways. We encourage activism but we condemn violent action. It is essential for me as a Nartist to spread awareness and to share with you what I recognize to be true.
33. We are for sustainability and the use of clean and renewable energy such as solar, wind, tidal, and

thermal energy, which we have an abundance of in nature, but which is not profitable to the rulers of the world: the CEOs of multinational corporations... the royal bloodlines and the hidden networks through which they manipulate. We are nature!

34. We are for a resource-based economy as opposed to the current outmoded monetary system, which was inherently designed to fail (through stock market crashes and great depressions) making profit only for the rich one percent over and over and over again.

35. We believe that education should be free and open to all; therefore, we gladly offer our knowledge to interested individuals and groups in a participatory-style workshop format. We love teaching because we love learning.

36. We are open to learn from all sorts of ancient spiritual traditions and contemporary scientific findings that are insightful.

37. We love our enemies not only our neighbors. And we whole-heartedly welcome any constructive criticism that can help us improve.

38. Human equality is unquestionable.

39. One of our goals as Nartists is to reconnect with our inner child just like Antoine de Saint-Exupéry did in *The Little Prince*.

40. A true Nartist is a student—and eventually a master—of the Art of Living, which is the enjoyment of the mundane (like washing the dishes, cooking, or gardening, etc.) as well as the

experience of the Divine through prayer, meditation, fasting, etc.

41. As Beings of Light, we are aware of the negative conspiracy theories that exist in our world today and we know that our strongest weapon against those who want to control us through fear is to spread LOVE through awareness and action. Because "love is the freedom from fear" as Krishnamurti put it.

Addendum

The Nartist Manifesto was written on 09/28/2011 (Chicago, IL) and revised on 03/03/2020 (Santa Fe, NM). I read the manifesto in public at the Southside Hub of Production (S.h.o.P.) in Hyde Park (Chicago, IL) on 11/06/2011. The Nartist Manifesto grew out of my frustration with the politics of art scenes around the world (i.e., the movers & shakers who get to define what constitutes 'art' or 'good' art). The Nartist Manifesto grew specifically out of an angry poem, it was my way of channeling my frustration into something playful because who writes manifestos these days anyways?

www.robertbeshara.com

BLESS
&
The Overgraduators

Seline Durrer
Silvia Fagniani
Ting Gong
Margaret Munchheimer
Marilyn Volkman
Joanne Vosloo

TEMPORARY EXHIBITION AGREEMENT CONTRACT
FOR
OVERGRADUATION

THE UNDERSIGNED:

_____

having its registered office/residing at

_____

(address, town/city, postcode)

HAS AGREED AS FOLLOWS

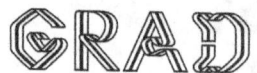

§1 IDENTITY

1.1 The undersigned will define itself, falling into the professional title or category of:

○ the **'artist'**
○ the **'craftsperson'**
○ the **'curator'**
○ other   _____

1.2 The undersigned herein agrees to identify with and sincerely develop the above indicated title for the duration of the exhibition.

1.3 All the undersigned hereinafter agree to engage the titles selected by the undersigned in §1 of each contract, with genuine curiosity for the duration of the exhibition.

1.4 Moreover, the undersigned hereby collectively agree to be referred to as 'The Overgraduates' for the duration of the exhibition and a self-determined period thereafter.

§2 PARTICIPATION

2.1 Participation shall commence on April 15, 2020. This contract will be signed and notarized for the purpose of regulating the participation in agreement with the MANIFESTO FOR OVERGRADUATION.

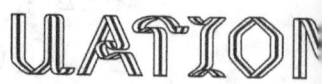

§3 TERM OF THE CONTRACT

3.1 This Temporary Exhibition Agreement Contract shall be concluded for a fixed term of 5 months and shall end on August 15, 2020 by lapse of time.

3.2 It is expressly stipulated that the undersigned may not terminate participation during the fixed-term of the Overgraduation exhibition unless prohibited by law or health, and the unexpected regulations or conditions that ensue from such legal or medical circumstances.

3.3 Moreover, it is expressly stipulated that any fixed-term participation may be terminated collectively by The Overgraduates if the undersigned violates the MANIFESTO FOR OVERGRADUATION which is valid and approved at that time, or if the undersigned consistently declines or fails to contribute with a genuine heart to the activities and exercises The Overgraduates have justifiably set into motion, based on the same manifesto.

§4 RESPONSIBILITIES

4.1 The undersigned will develop said professional identities [see § 1.1] for the duration of the contract, and will advance with demonstrable contribution to the strength of the exhibition and relevance to the future of the undersigned's work.

4.2 The undersigned will remain open and engaged in critical feedback and reflection with The Overgraduates' in accordance with the MANIFESTO FOR OVERGRADUATION.

4.3 The undersigned will hereby contribute to the strength of the exhibition, as the exhibition will contribute to the strength of undersigned.

4.4 Hereinafter, The Overgraduates will collaborate to ensure the relevance of the exhibition contents and programming including, but not limited to, its objects, services, events and documents. Relevance is defined and described in the MANIFESTO FOR OVERGRADUATION to be attached hereto as an annex and to be initiated by all parties.

§5 RENUMERATION

5.1 Undersigned shall receive a one-time payment of € 2580, equal to one year EU Sandberg Instituut tuition.

5.2 The Overgraduates may approve an additional 2 special payments to each undersigned participant upon completion of 'exceptional objects, services, documents or events' as defined in the MANIFESTO FOR OVERGRADUATION.

§6 WORKING HOURS

6.2 The undersigned may distribute their weekly working hours at their own discretion, but in compliance with "The Overgraduate Code" [see Annex 2].

6.3 Moreover, the undersigned agrees to be present and available for open office ours, meetings, exercises and public activities as justifiably scheduled and set into motion by The Overgraduates.

§7 MANIFESTO

7.1 The undersigned undertakes to comply with the MANIFESTO FOR OVERGRADUATION, in particular the declarations regarding "Values for Temporary Exhibition", "The Overgraduate Code", "Real World Relevance", "Conflict of Interest" and "Made to Measure Professions", as valid and approved at the time.

7.2 The MANIFESTO FOR OVERGRADUATION and declarations are attached hereto as Annex 1–2. A copy of the manifesto, as amended by The Overgraduates will be routinely published on the Internet and is available for inspection with The Overgraduates during open office hours [see § 6] .

7.3 The undersigned acknowledges that The Overgraduates, a collective to which the undersigned conditionally belongs, may amend the manifesto and declarations at any time.

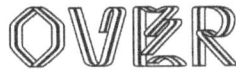

THIS DOCUMENT HAS BEEN SUB- MITTED FOR THIS PUBLICATION ON FRIDAY 20TH OF MARCH 2020.

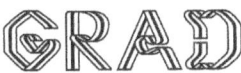

THE DOCUMENT IS A PROACTIVE ELEMENT IN THE PROJECT "OVER- GRADUATION" AND DEVELOPED IN RELATION WITH THE INVITA- TION OF HET NIEUWE INSTITUUT, ROTTERDAM, THE NETHERLANDS TO PRODUCE AN EXHIBITION ABOUT VALUES.

DUE TO THE CURRENT SITUATION WITH CORONAVIRUS THE "OVER- GRADUATORS" PROJECT GROUP IS WORKING REMOTELY FROM HOMES ALL OVER EUROPE.

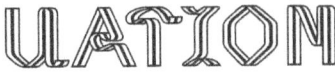

The core group members are:
SILVIA FAGNIANI (IT)
SELINE DURRER (CH)
MARILYN VOLKMAN (US)
MARGARET MUNCHHEIMER (US)
TING GONG (CN)
JOANNE VOSLOO (NL)
BLESS (FR/D)

Graphic Design by Studio Manuel Raeder

Jessica Charlesworth
&
Tim Parsons

SANDCASTLE MAKER

The Sandcastle Maker was designed by Henry Ingham, (Tim Parsons' great grandfather), probably in the 1940s. He was an engineer in a cotton mill in Lancashire, England so would have had a good understanding of how technical things worked, especially tools like lathes. The Sandcastle maker can be seen as a lathe for sand.

The version shown here was exhibited at the Spectacular Vernacular exhibition at The Chicago Cultural Center, and is made from 1/2 inch plywood and 3/4 inch dowel. If you want to make your own, follow the drawings on page 41 to cut out the pieces. We have not included the blade shape because we thought you might like to design your own. It just needs a 3/4 inch hole near one end so it can be attached to the rest of the tool.

You will need two of component A, and one each of B and C. You will also need a 3/4 inch dowel of approximately 24 inches and another short piece roughly 2 inches long.

When you have cut out the components and drilled the holes in components A and C you can assemble parts A and B together. Sandwich part B between the two As so it resembles the drawing. Glue these parts together. Once the glue has dried, drill a 3/4 inch hole down through the top of this assembly of parts (see drawing).

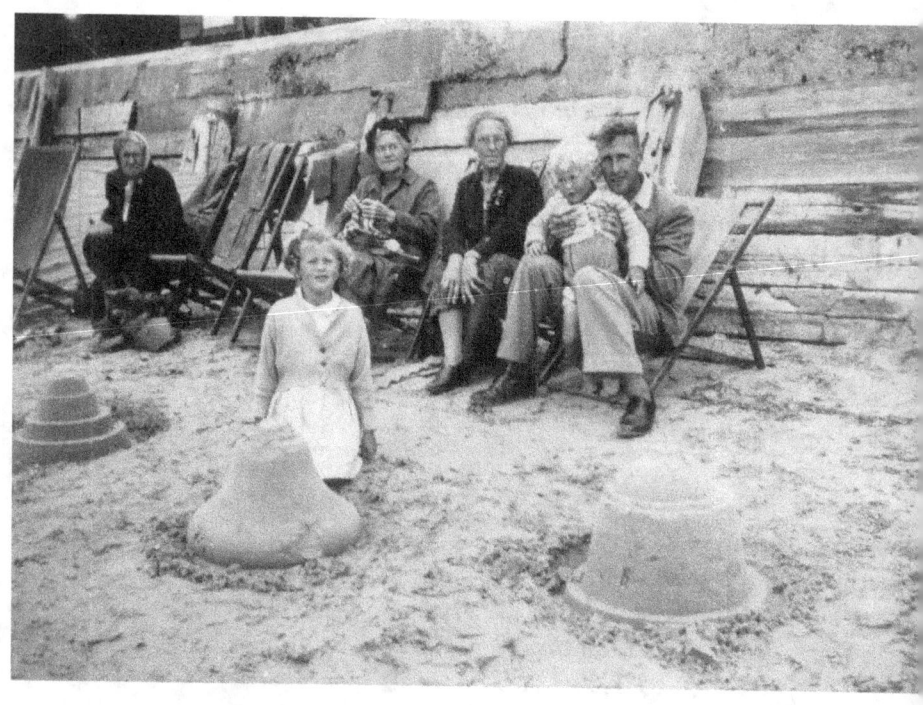

Fig. 1, Tim Parsons' family on a beach in the Isle of
Wight, UK in 1948.

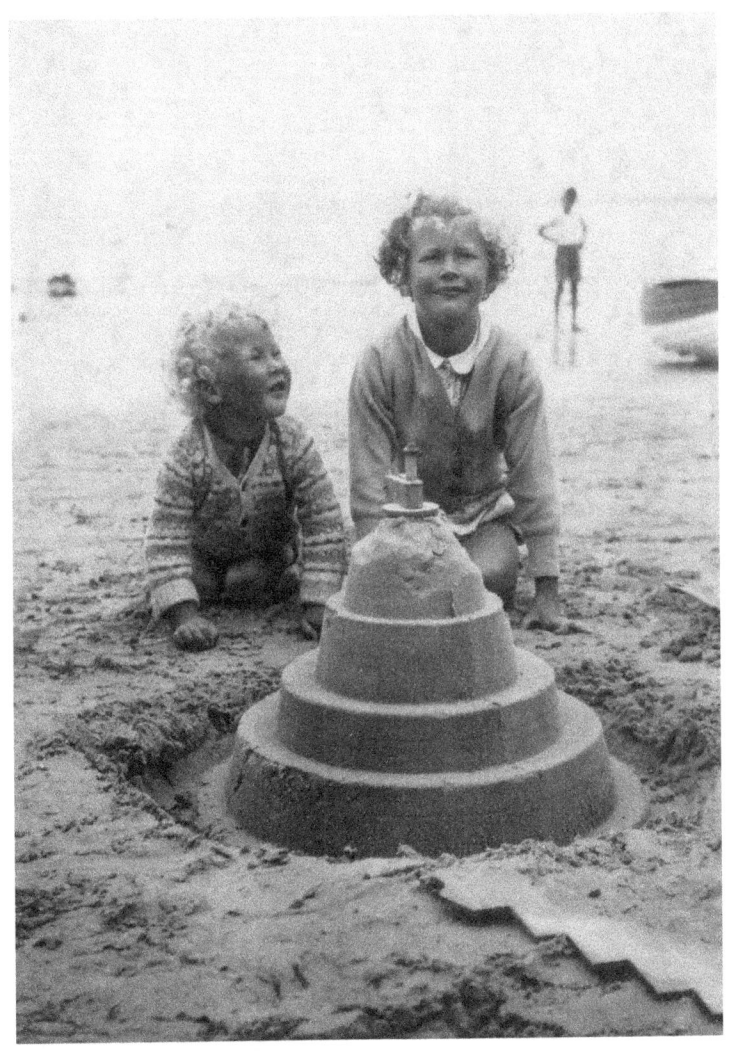

Fig. 2, Tim Parsons' mother Dorothy Parsons and
uncle Mike Ingham

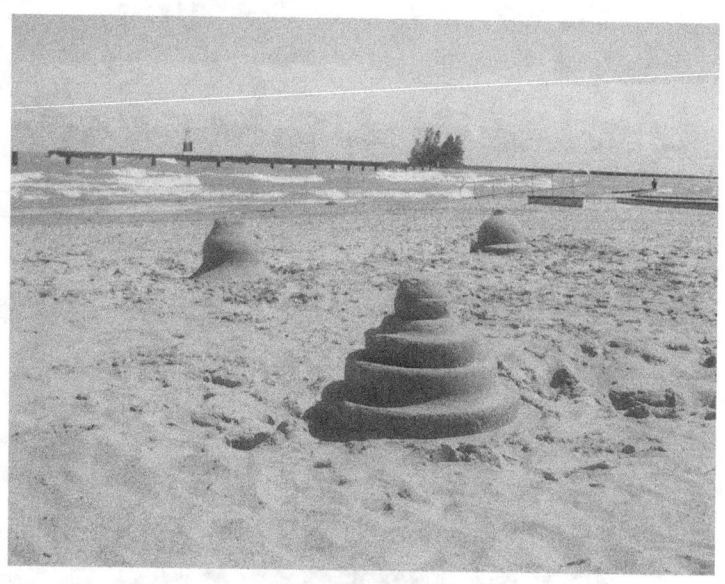

Fig. 3, Sandcastles made on North Avenue Beach by
SAIC students.

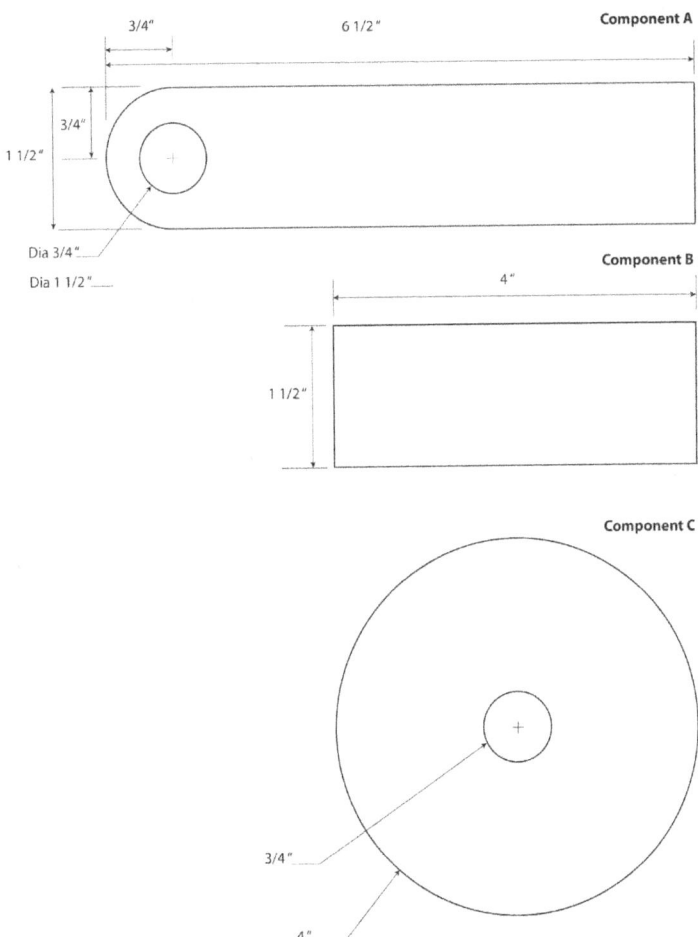

Component A

3/4"   6 1/2"

3/4"

1 1/2"

Dia 3/4"

Dia 1 1/2"

Component B

4"

1 1/2"

Component C

3/4"

4"

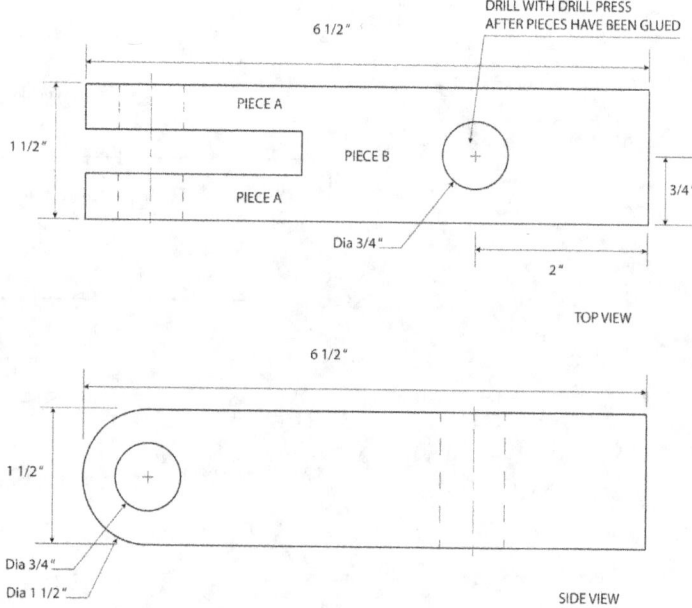

6 1/2"

DRILL WITH DRILL PRESS
AFTER PIECES HAVE BEEN GLUED

PIECE A

1 1/2"

PIECE B

PIECE A

3/4"

Dia 3/4"

2"

TOP VIEW

6 1/2"

1 1/2"

Dia 3/4"

Dia 1 1/2"

SIDE VIEW

HINGE PIECE, ASSEMBLED DIMENSIONS

SANDCASTLE MAKER ASSEMBLY

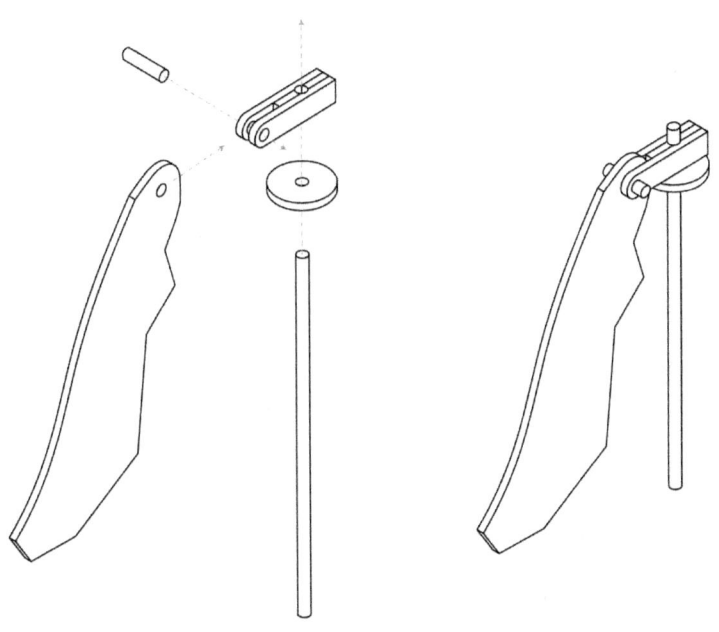

Alex DeGraaf

PFv7.3.4

Pastel Fractal's mission is to perform wonders 🐚 *with the mission statements*

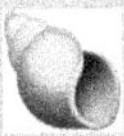

of Chicagoans.

Alexander DeGraaf's mission is to research for Pastel Fractal.

Alexander DeGraaf **primarily researches by means of interactive research installations such as the one pictured below** titled *PFv7.3.4* which collects the mission-statement data of Chicagoans.
Based on the research of Alexander DeGraaf, the tools

and materials of this installation are optimal in order for Pastel Fractal to perform wonders 🐚 with the mission statements of Chicagoans.

The colored lights on the installation flash when Pastel Fractal changes from processing the data from one interface to another. The four corresponding colors, interfaces, and research prompts are the following: **State!** (PINK) *"State a mission of yours as a Chicagoan."* Participants interface with a 15-year-old notebook computer and "Notepad" program to store data to floppy disks which are sent sliding through the installation to be processed on the opposite side.

Sing! (ORANGE) *"Type out the words to a song about accessibility as a Chicagoan."*
Participants interface with a 25-year-old digital word processor to store data to floppy disks which are sent sliding through the installation to be processed on the opposite side.

Promote! (GREEN) *"Promote a mission of yours as a Chicagoan."*
Participants interface with a 4-year-old tablet (which is screen-mirrored to a child-size karaoke machine on the opposite side of the installation) and then send blank floppy disks sliding through the installation to the opposite side.

Rage! (BLUE) *"Write a restriction of yours as a Chicagoan."*
Participants interface with a silver marker to write data on uncased floppy disks which are sent sliding through the installation to be processed on the opposite side

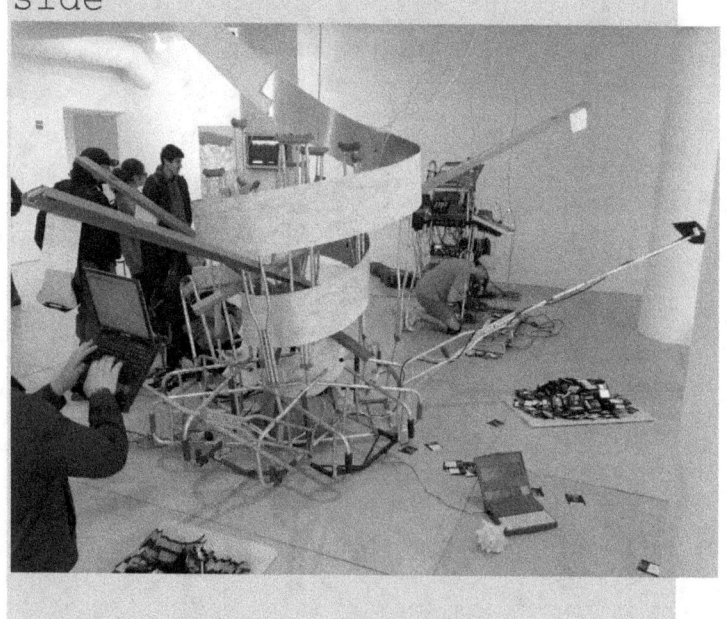

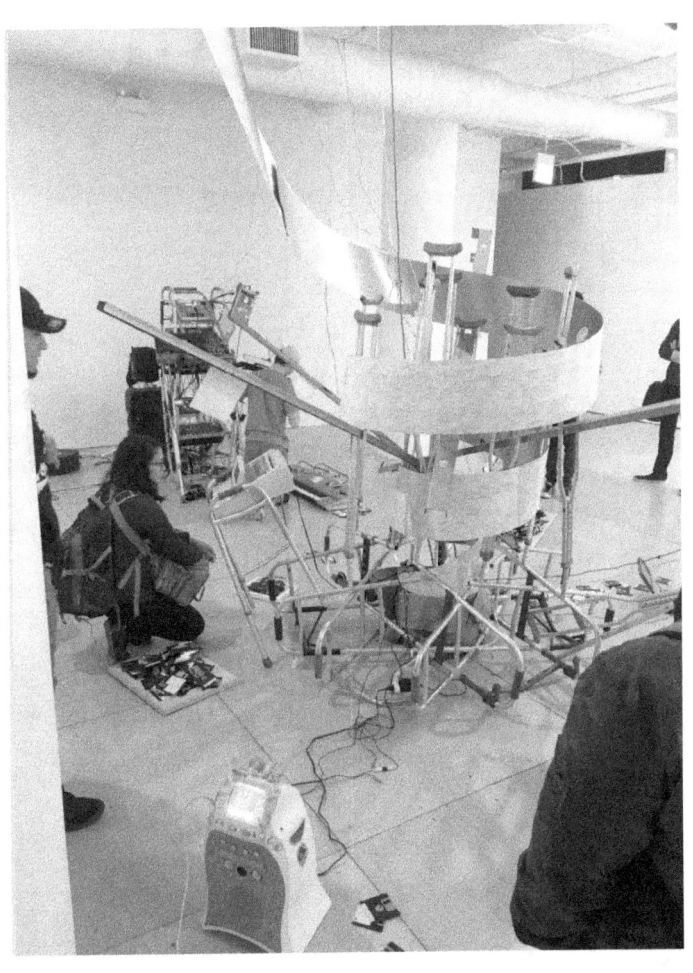

Wonders are qualified by positive experience beyond understanding.

Tiny Domingos

The Oak and the Reed

The Oak spoke one day to the Reed
"You have good reason to complain;
A Wren for you is a load indeed;
The smallest wind bends you in twain.
You are forced to bend your head;
While my crown faces the plains
And not content to block the sun
Braves the efforts of the rains.
What for you is a North Wind is for me
but a zephyr.
Were you to grow within my shade
Which covers the whole neighbourhood
You'd have no reason to be afraid
For I would keep you from the storm.
Instead you usually grow
In places humid, where the winds doth
blow.
Nature to thee hath been unkind."
"Your compassion", replied the Reed
"Shows a noble character indeed;
But do not worry: the winds for me
Are much less dangerous than for thee;
I bend, not break. You have 'til now
Resisted their great force unbowed,
But beware.
As he said these very words
A violent angry storm arose.
The tree held strong; the Reed he bent.
The wind redoubled and did not relent,
Until finally it uprooted the poor Oak
Whose head had been in the heavens
And roots among the dead folk.

(Translation by Michael Star)

le Chêne et le Roseau

Le Chêne un jour dit au Roseau :
"Vous avez bien sujet d'accuser la Nature ;
Un Roitelet pour vous est un pesant fardeau.
Le moindre vent, qui d'aventure
Fait rider la face de l'eau,
Vous oblige à baisser la tête :
Cependant que mon front, au Caucase pareil,
Non content d'arrêter les rayons du soleil,
Brave l'effort de la tempête.
Tout vous est Aquilon, tout me semble Zéphyr.
Encor si vous naissiez à l'abri du feuillage
Dont je couvre le voisinage,
Vous n'auriez pas tant à souffrir :
Je vous défendrais de l'orage ;
Mais vous naissez le plus souvent
Sur les humides bords des Royaumes du vent.
La nature envers vous me semble bien injuste.
- Votre compassion, lui répondit l'Arbuste,
Part d'un bon naturel ; mais quittez ce souci.
Les vents me sont moins qu'à vous redoutables.
Je plie, et ne romps pas. Vous avez jusqu'ici
Contre leurs coups épouvantables
Résisté sans courber le dos ;
Mais attendons la fin. "Comme il disait ces mots,
Du bout de l'horizon accourt avec furie
Le plus terrible des enfants
Que le Nord eût portés jusque-là dans ses flancs.
L'Arbre tient bon ; le Roseau plie.
Le vent redouble ses efforts,
Et fait si bien qu'il déracine
Celui de qui la tête au Ciel était voisine
Et dont les pieds touchaient à l'Empire des
Morts.

Jean de la Fontaine

ART AND CURATORIAL PRACTICE AS RESILIENCE

panta rhei: Greek quotation attributed to Heracleitus
Definition of panta rhei: all things are in flux

Merian-Webster dictionary

"Fall seven times, stand up eight."
Japanese Proverb

"RISK EXPOSURE" was the title of a solo exhibition I presented one year ago in Porto, Portugal. The show brought together digital graphics - which referred to the visualization of data flows and to risk management - and sculptural elements - which pointed to precarious or unlikely balances - in a large in situ installation. A title that now gains a new reading: as I write these lines (mid March 2020) the world lives a very particular situation: the Coronavirus pandemic (COVID-19) has spread to all continents and is threatening the lives of millions of people. Initially relativized by decision-makers, the pandemic is spreading at a great speed, leading to the unprecedented closure of borders and to seclusion at home. Italy is one of the countries where the situation is most worrying. Precisely the country to which I have travelled regularly in the last two years and which I have come to know much better through a vast SciArt project. The basic idea of this project - entitled "LANDSLIDE (Resilience in Unstable Times)" - was to use the phenomenon of landslides as a metaphor for an era marked by rising populism and the consequent erosion of democratic values, as well as the mistrust and disinterest of various political leaders towards science and culture. Focusing mainly on the southern flank of the Eurozone - the most weak in geological, seismic and economic terms-, I have drawn a parallel between "geological collapse" (for example a landslide triggered by a seismic tremor) and "economic collapse". This led me to carry out the public artwork "The Price of Volatility" (Image 7) inspired by the upward and downward curve of a 3D chart representing the 10 years evolution of maturity bonds of Portugal, Spain and Italy (Greece had to be left out for breaking the scale!). A piece which gives tangibility to the Euro Debt Crisis (2010/11) which has seriously shaken the economic foundations of the so-called PIGS countries.

The study of the millenary cultures of the Mediterranean allows one to think in terms of millennial time and to contextualize their various cycles. After a downward cycle, another upward cycle follows. Italy is, par excellence, the European country of landslides, whose annual costs represent the greatest financial burden in terms of natural disasters. Speaking with specialists in Earth Sciences the notion of *panta rhei* ("Everything flows") attributed to Heracleitus was often adressed. The ground and the landscape itself are often seen as something solid and immutable, but the reality is that everything is in motion: tectonic plates, mountains slopes, rock falls, volcanoes like Stromboli and Etna, etc. The landscape of the transalpine peninsula illustrates this notion quite well and its hills and mountains often evoke the undulation of the sea. The whole geo-morphological movements, earthquakes, floods, the danger of volcanic eruptions and tsunamis represent a great challenge in terms of civil protection and cultural heritage. Italy has a big expertise in the field of geohazards and a close collaboration exists between Earth Science experts, cultural heritage managers and civil protection services. An interdisciplinary intermeshing that recalls the universalist spirit of the Renaissance and which is of the utmost importance to face the complexity of today's challenges. In fact, during my research in Italy I have come across unprecedented disciplinary crossroads with the same neuralgic point in the centre: the Italian Renaissance, which in turn, in various ways, re-reads Classical Antiquity and which transports the observer into a very broad time dimension as if it were a long succession of mirrors.

A golden moment of the Renaissance: the introduction of perspective in painting - based on a new application of geometric concepts - opens a new page in art history not only in terms of spatial illusion but also because all layers of society could understand it regardless of their education. The landscape starts to play a more important role until it becomes autonomous. Geology and anatomy will later be born from this élan. Today ancient prints and Renaissance paintings are part of a scientific database that makes it possible to understand the geo-morphological mouvements of San Leo in the historical region of Montefeltro (Northern Apennines, Italy).

A beautiful journey that will be etched in my memory: from Lake Maggiore to Sicily returning by Craco (a town that had to be evacuated in the 80es due to an irreversible landslide), by San Leo (a real castle in the air) and closing with a golden key in Arezzo and Urbino on the steps of Piero della Francesca, solar painter and author of the legendary treaty "De Prospectiva pingendi" (On the Perspective of painting). Unforgettable was also the stay at Stromboli and the observation of the flank collapse (which gave rise to a short video with this title). I could spend hours here rambling on the charms of Italy and its dazzling cultural riches, but I take this opportunity to express all my solidarity with the patients and with the families of the thousands of people who have died in the pandemic. The Italian people have repeatedly shown its resilience and I am sure that Italy will stand up with even more impetus after this difficult period.

The notion of panta rhei underlines the importance of flows which can be found in the most diverse areas: virology, geophysics, vulcanology, economics, communication, transportation, etc. I invite the reader to reflect on this notion of flow. George Steiner was critical of hyper-specialization because it prevents dialogue between people from different areas. I share his opinion and think it is important to enhance cooperation and dialogue between artistic and scientific research.

Finally, agility can be a vital asset: against all appearances, it is the reed that proves resilience and not the portentous oak in the fable of Jean de La Fontaine. Created without great funds, nor a powerful support network, ROSALUX is an Berlin based artist run space, in which artistic production, presentation and reflection take place independently of commercial or institutional criteria. With a program that started at the end of 2006, ROSALUX has the merit of continuing to serve as a presentation platform for international and local artists, despite the current gentrification processes in Berlin and the chronic lack of structural funding. ROSALUX is now considered an integral part of the Berlin independent scene. Being agile does not mean bowing before someone else. Apparently the reed bends according to the wind, but in fact it follows a logic well adapted to its terrain, which allows it to face a whole series of storms and finally be the most resilient. Isn't artistic creation also an act of resistance? Where does the energy for such tenacity come from? Curiosity, passion for art and a great investment in terms of work are energy resources that move mountains.

The final message of this text could not be simpler: current times are unstable and the way to resilience involves new developments in Art and Science. Not their abandonment. Make bridges not walls!

List of figures on next three pages

6. "projectedspace: Florence", Tiny Domingos 2019,
digital photography /

7. "THE PRICE OF VOLATILITY", Tiny Domingos, 2019, Joint
Research Center of the European Commission, Ispra, Italy Nylon
sailcloth, jersey barriers, steel structure and cables, 31,20 x 6,22 x 4,50
m. Photo Credits: Ulrike Bausch

8. "RISK EXPOSURE", Tiny Domingos, 2019
Solo show at Espaço Mira, March 2019, Porto, Portugal.

9. "LOOKING FOR FREEDOM", João Pombeiro, 2007
Solo show at ROSALUX, 2007 Berlin. Curated by Tiny Domingos.
Photo credits: TD

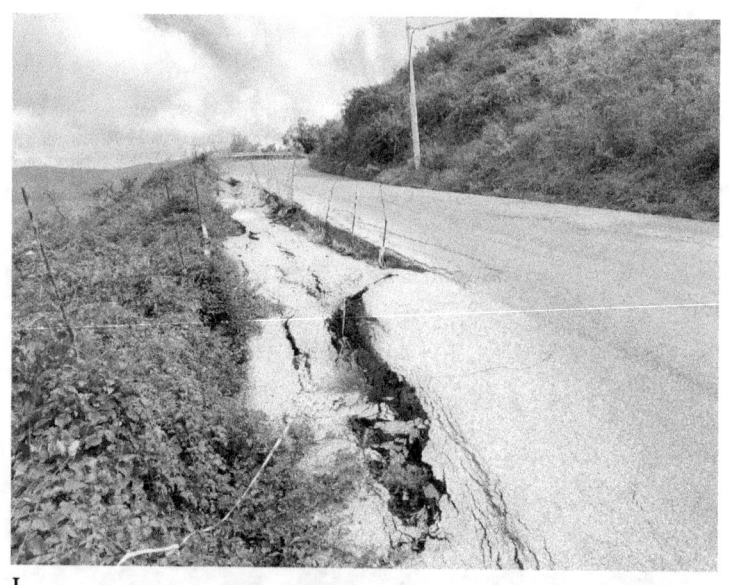

I

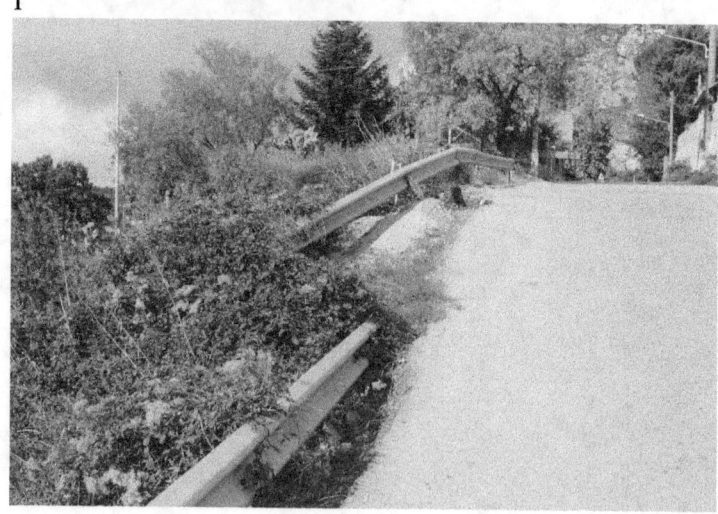

2

58

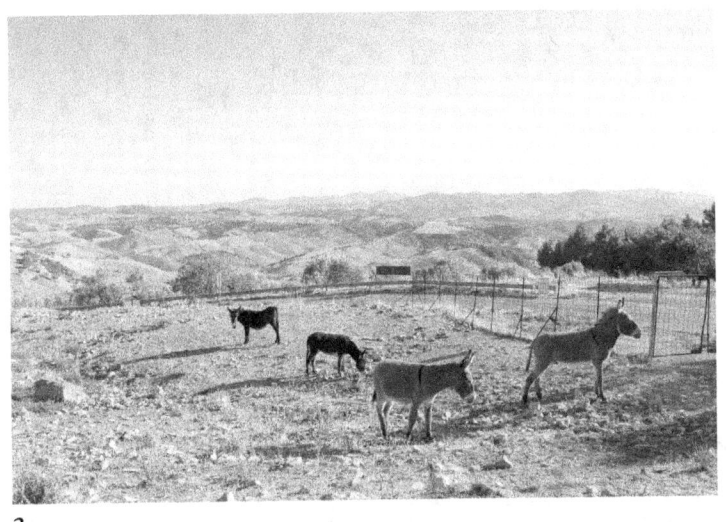

3

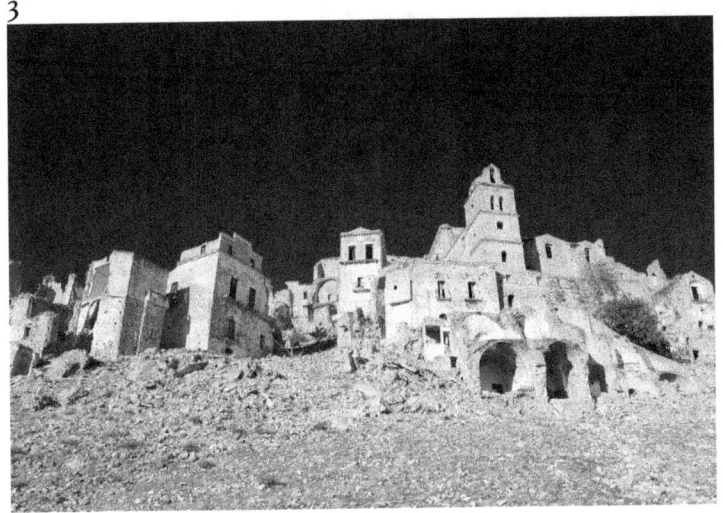

4

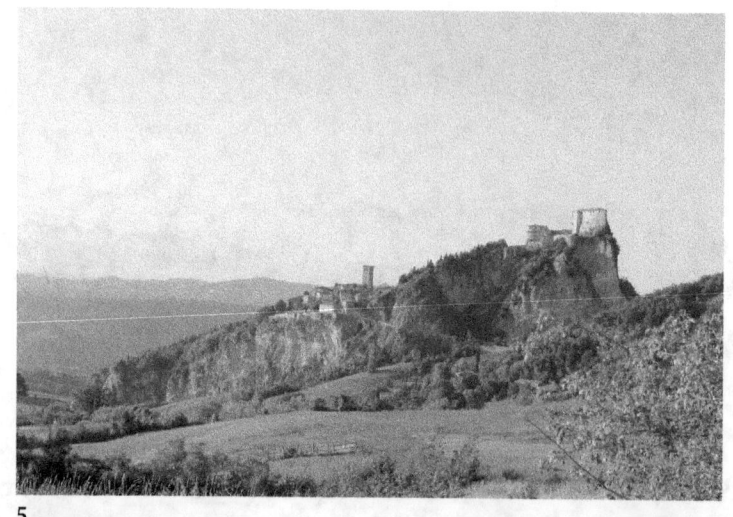

5

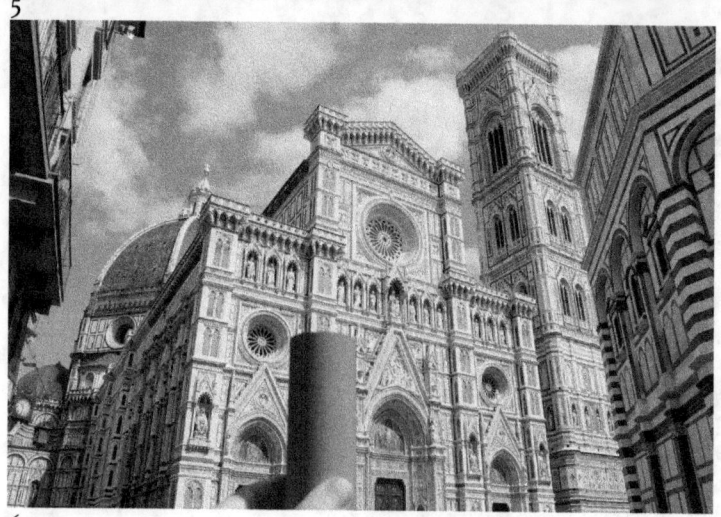

6

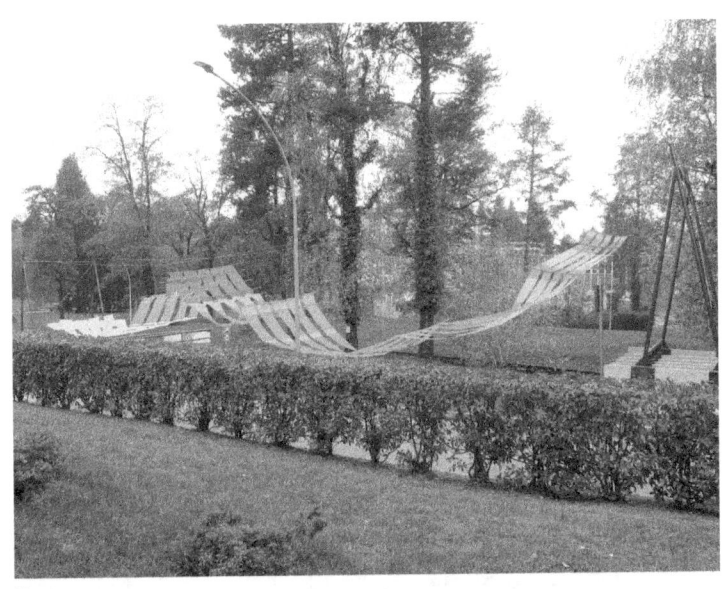

7

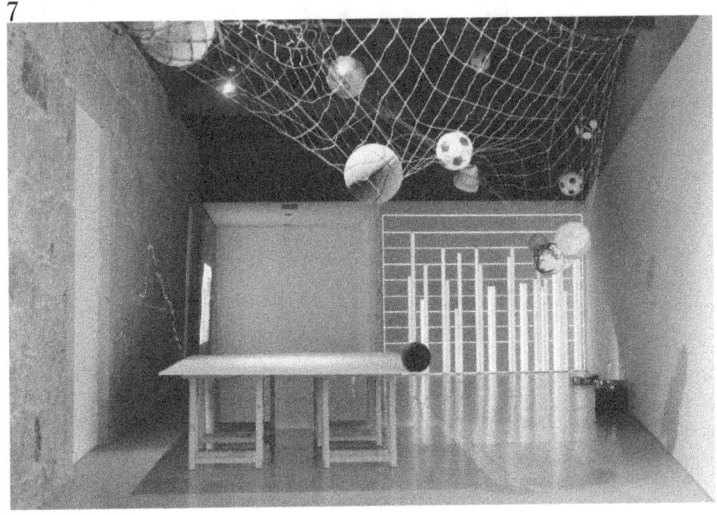

8

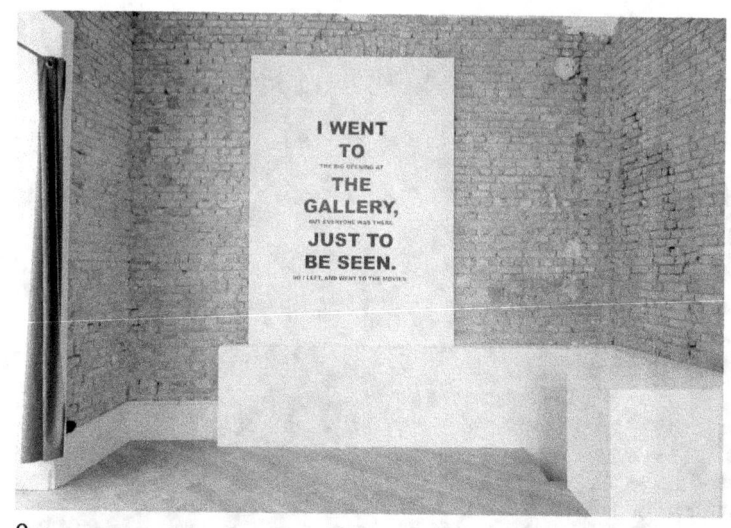

9

Rachel Epp Buller

Lessons in Care curriculum
March 2020

Dear friends,
I invite you to think with me about a connection between handwritten letters and relations of care. Writing a letter by hand forces us to slow down, to take time, to take care with the words and for the receiver.

For one week (or longer if you wish), I invite you to spend up to 20 minutes each day writing something by hand to someone who is or has been in your extended circle of caring relations. Think broadly about this circle: child, partner, childhood friend, parent or grandparent (living or deceased), a friend or partner with whom you've lost touch but once shared an important connection; think also about the possibilities of multispecies care – writing to an animal, or to a particular place. What you write is up to you; perhaps it is a thank-you note of sorts, acknowledging a way that you have received care in the relationship, but it need not be an expression of gratitude necessarily. Caring relationships are complicated, after all.

These words can be many or few, written on stationery, a postcard, a post-it note, a receipt, a leaf, whatever seems most appropriate to the words and the recipient.

Caring relations are often part of an invisible labor, so I invite you to change that by sharing documentation of your gestures in a public way of your choosing. (If Instagram is your medium of choice, please tag me @rebuller74 and hashtag #lessonsincare.)

Take care,

Rachel Epp Buller

Tony Foley

Taking Names

Learning the names of those who live and work around us is an essential part of humanizing our community. Whether family, friends, neighbors, workers, regulars, elected officials, houseless people --- every name has a story behind it and you are part of that story. It's time to take stock.

1. Name as many people as you can that live in a one mile radius from where you live

_____   _____   _____
_____   _____   _____
_____   _____   _____
_____   _____   _____

2. Describe as many people as you can whose names you do not yet know that live within one mile of you

_____   _____   _____
_____   _____   _____
_____   _____   _____
_____   _____   _____

3. Name as many people as you have spoken to within the last two weeks

_____   _____   _____
_____   _____   _____
_____   _____   _____
_____   _____   _____
_____   _____   _____

Conrad Freiburg

All I Seek
March 15 2020

Trust yourself and your embodied wisdom.
Get by with less.
Learn to forage.
Its okay to be sad.
Even better to be happy.
Find friends who know more than you do.
Pay attention to your body,
even more to your feeling.
Create a sacred place, even if its an unfolded
bandana on a plank of wood.
Tell your story in the best way you know how.
Work to accept the world the way it is, and humbly
offer your alternative.
Hold yourself with kindness,
your enemies with compassion,
your loved ones with presence.

Learn to take your heart out of your chest and hold
it like a newborn. Thank it with a
lullaby song for being so strong,
and for beating even though you didn't ask it to.

Honor the people who give attention to you, and
love you as you fumble for meaning on a
bandstand, white wall, hard drive, or on a small
table.

Show the squares how beautiful not having an edge
can be;
Unlimited in ambiguiity,
specific,
careful,
so vague there is room for us all.
So easy, kind, true
that it is unknowable some of the time.

Perfection is the booby prize.
Desire is a universal fuel,
returning to us like the air we breathe.
Only a little will is required to
inhale deep.
"all is welcome"
Is all I seek.

Matthew Girson

How to be in it, nothing more, nothing less

If today is a weekday then face north or south.
If today is a weekend then face east or west.
If the month ends in the letter "y" then take very
short steps very slowly.
If the month ends in the letter "r" then walk
normally.
If the month ends in another letter then walk
briskly.
If it is clear sky then walk alone.
If there are any clouds with no precipitation then
invite a friend.
Continue for 30 minutes to four hours.
If the temperature is below freezing then continue
on a bicycle or in a car.
If the temperature is between 33F and 75F then
continue in a car or on a train.
If the temperature is above 76F then continue on a
train or on a plane.
When you get hungry, turn left, find a place to eat,
enjoy a meal and then continue in the same
direction via the same means of transportation.
When you have to urinate, continue straight, find a
suitable place to relieve yourself and do so, and
then continue in the same direction via the same
means of transportation.
When you have to defecate, turn right, find a
suitable place to relieve yourself and do so, and
then continue in the same direction via the same
means of transportation.

When you are tired, then rest until you feel restored and continue in the same direction via the same means of transportation.

When you move from one municipality to another, turn left or right.

When you move from one state to another, send a postcard to someone you care about. Write the following on the back of the postcard, "I am on a journey with no destinations."

When you move from one country to another, send a postcard to someone you care about. Write the following on the back of the postcard, "My journey continues with no destination."

When you get to an insurmountable obstacle, then turn around and follow the prompts above.

Continue to send postcards with either text above to people you care about and people you don't.

Send them at random points on your journeys in between your destinations.

The journeys end only when you say they have ended, not before, not after.

The destinations are places to start, nothing more, nothing less.

Shawn Greene

CARRARIUM

★ SELF CONTAINED CAR GREEN HOUSE

GLASS ROOF
Lets in the suns heat and light.

IRRIGATION SYSTEM
Rain water is captured and stored and irrigates via 12 volt pump.

SOLAR POWER
- runs irrigation pumps, fans, etc.

ONBOARD COMPOST
- Put in the scraps and let the worms do the rest!

Ryan Griffis

HOW TO DRAW LINES ON THE GROUND IN A FLOODPLAIN, AND WATCH THEM BE WASHED AWAY

1) Read the following excerpt from the 1967 poem "Lake Superior" by Lorine Niedecker.

Iron the common element of earth
in rocks and freighters

Sault Sainte Marie—big boats
coal-black and iron-ore-red
topped with what white castlework

The waters working together
*   internationally*
Gulls playing both sides

2) Fill in the map provided with the following information, using writing and/or drawing:
• What do you know about the atmosphere above you, right now? Can you describe what it is composed of? What lives there? What is your relationship to it, and it to you?
• What do you know about the earth and water beneath you, right now? Can you describe what it is composed of? What lives there? What is your relationship to it, and it to you?
• Imagine this same atmosphere, earth and water as far back in time as you can. Answer the same questions.
• Imagine this same atmosphere, earth and water as far ahead in time as you can. Answer the same questions.

500 YEARS AHEAD

PRESENT

500 YEARS AGO

65536 feet

16 feet

2 feet

YOU

LAND SURFACE

1 foot

4 feet

256 feet

Judith Heineman

Bringing your Audience onto the Stage and into Your Story

One of comedian W.C. Fields' (1880 - 1946) most famous quotes was, "Never work with animals or children," although he secretly admired children according to his IMDb biography.

That was a warning to theater actors who would often be upstaged by them. However, if you want to shine a spotlight on your story and have keen attention paid, I strongly urge you to intentionally bring children onto the stage with you! When you bring adults or children literally into your story there is a hyper focus from family and friends in the audience to see what they are doing. The audience is sitting on the edge of their chairs, snapping pictures of course. It is also exciting and fun for the teller to have a bit of unpredictability in the performance and keeps the retelling fresh. Selecting these living "characters" can vary from simply asking for volunteers in the moment, or if you want a bit more control, asking teachers to identify cooperative students in advance if in a school setting.

Once these strangers are standing next to you, populating your story, how can you seamlessly make them part of the tale? Preparation is all. Know your story so well, that you have planned numerous places where you can feed them lines from the story quickly and easily, shifting the microphone back and forth between you. I have found that this technique works particularly well in outdoor festivals when there are more distractions and concentration is harder.

You can give stage directions audibly such as, "use a deep voice, whisper, or say these lines together," if you want more than one person to speak simultaneously, perhaps as animal characters. In addition, you can turn to the general audience and have them speak words or phrases in unison expanding the story even more. There are times when I needed only one character, pointed to the child in the audience I thought I had selected, but two came up. I never send one back, but just make two of that character work like "The Magic Pot!" So, if you have always stood on stage alone speaking the words of various characters, delineating them by shifting body language, tone, pacing, etc., this technique might be an enjoyable change of pace.

In closing, not only did the W. C. Field quote resonate, but I also kept hearing the snarky lyrics to the clever 1930's Noel Coward patter song, "Don't put your Daughter on the Stage, Mrs. Worthington. . . I'm on my knees, Mrs, Worthington, please Mrs. Worthington, don't put your daughter on the stage!" I am proposing just the opposite, but nevertheless, try to find it and give it a listen.

Judith Heineman, Storyteller
Juhestories@aol.com

Hannah Hirsekorn

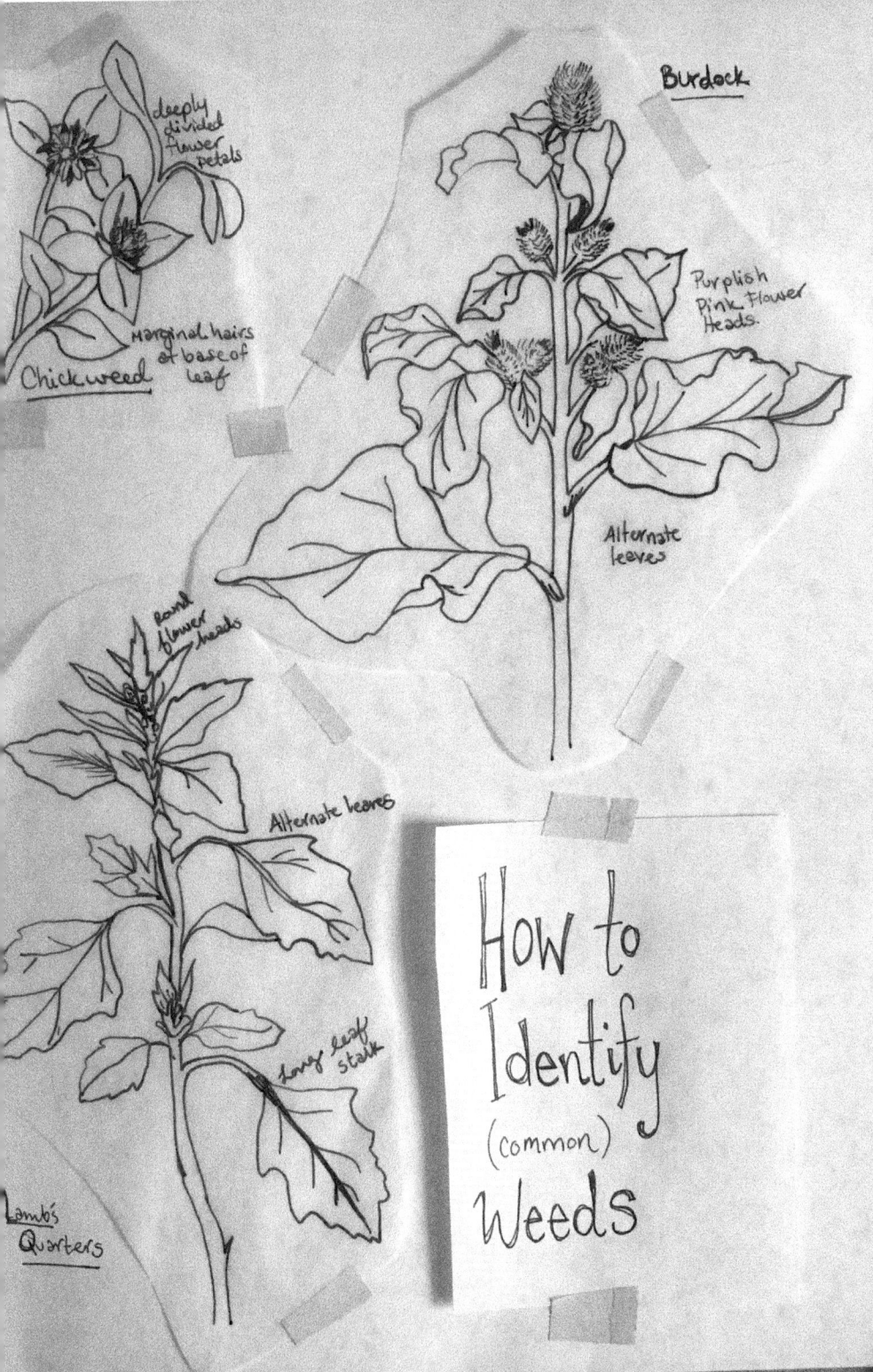

deeply divided flower petals

Burdock

Purplish Pink Flower Heads.

marginal hairs at base of leaf

Chickweed

Alternate leaves

Round flower heads

Alternate leaves

long leaf stalk

Lamb's Quarters

How to Identify (common) Weeds

Sorrel

3 lobed leaf

Arrow shaped leaves

leaves edible before flowers emerge

spreading roots Rhizomes

Dandelio

leafless hollow flower stal

Lobed leaf pointed 'lion's

Nettles

paired leaves (opposite)

spiny hairs - will sting!

Horizontal rhizome

Pur

sm

leaves witho stalk

Plant is Smooth & succulent

sprawlin ground

Brian Holmes

Southeast Chicago

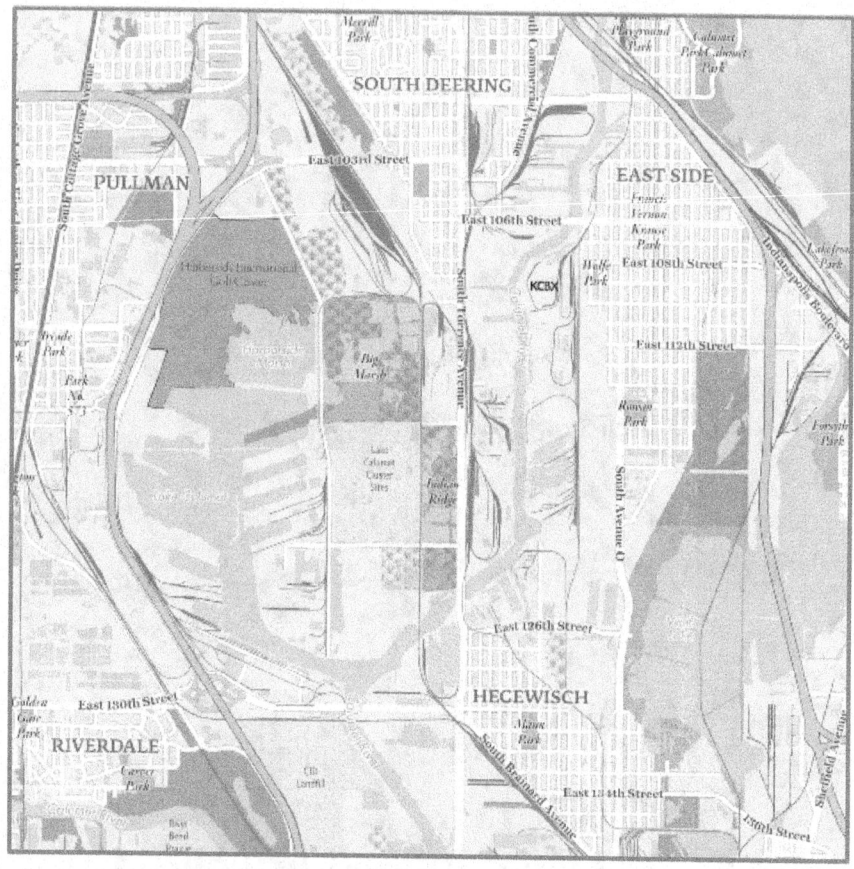

Is it a neighborhood? an industrial corridor? a river
basin? an oil refinery? a steel mill? a recycling center?
a scrap heap? a port? a wetland? a skate park?
a chemical dump? an urban wilderness?
a sacrifice zone? a restorable future?

The Anthropocene Begins in Your Town

Background
Formerly a vast wetland, Southeast Chicago
became a focus of intense industrial activity from
early 1880s
onward, when the South Works of the North
Chicago Rolling Mill (later US Steel) was installed
near the mouth of the Calumet River. In 1890
Standard Oil of Indiana opened a refinery in
nearby Whiting (now BP). The Calumet-
Saganashkee Channel gave the oil, steel and
chemical industries of Southeast Chicago a direct
link to the Mississippi River system in 1922, and the
Port of Chicago took its contemporary form on
Lake Calumet in 1959. But after two more decades
of tapering growth, the industries along the banks
of the Calumet suddenly collapsed in the 1980s.
The ruins have not yet been fully cleared. Today, as
fragments of the wetlands are slowly restored, the
area appears as a living and often densely
inhabited monument to the advent of the
Anthropocene.

Four sites
We'll drive over the Indiana Tollway bridge,
catching a view of the mouth of the Calumet River,
directly below, as well as the BP refinery and the
still-functioning Arcelor-Mittal steel complex in

87

East Chicago, to the left. Then we'll go down to the streets of Southeast Chicago. If all goes well (weather, etc), we will visit four sites:

- *The 106th street bridge, where you can see recycling industries, barge traffic, river ports, and above all the Koch Brothers' KCBX terminal, whose gigantic open pile of dusty petcoke was shut down by community activism in 2016, but without entirely stopping the direct rail-to-barge transfer of this noxious Tar Sands by-product.*

- *The new park of Big Marsh, between the river and the lake, where you might glimpse a bald eagle, or Chicago's highest mountain (the Paxton II landfill), or maybe even some skateborders and dirt bikers. Right next to them, invisible, are the Calumet Cluster sites – four chemical dumps that were the object of emergency interventions in the 1980s and were finally made a Superfund site in 2010, but without full cleanup yet, due to lack of funds...*

- *The Method plant in Pullman, on the west side of the lake, which makes Ecover soap products and presents the image of a clean, contemporary form of industrial manufacturing which, if replicated, might offer jobs to thousands of unemployed and underemployed inhabitants of Southeast Chicago.*

- Finally, the Southeast Environment Task Force, where artist Terry Evans will show images of the ongoing petcoke struggle and director Peggy Salazar will speak about the challenges that the local community faces, as well as the vision they have been developing for a sustainable redevelopment of the area. It's worth knowing that as residents concerned about the fate of their community, the members of SETF have helped to stop an airport, a coal gasification plant, a dump, a cement kiln, a police firing range and a tremendously stinky animal-feed plant, all in hopes of someday reaching their goal, which is a healthy place to live, work and raise the next generation.

Something to ponder
Why care about Southeast Chicago, or any other declining rustbelt district? One of the key concepts of political ecology is negative externalities. They're the environmental and social costs left off the account books of privately-owned production, whether it's toxic wastes, or damaged workers, or degraded land, or the very ruins of abandoned industry that no one bothers to clean up. These are said to be the crimes of capital, and I agree. But here's something I wonder about: to the extent that the so-called middle classes have been shaped in our very subjectivities by the affordances of privately-owned industrial production, don't we

have an existential interest in meeting, in knowing, in transforming those aspects of our own lives that we have left external to ourselves? Could that encounter be a strangely familiar way to become something fundamentally different? And perhaps to gain new powers, of a different order than those we have formerly possessed? For the inhabitants of colonial and neocolonial societies, this quest for self-knowledge might take you far afield, toward distant consequences of capitalist production. That voyage is important, without any doubt. But the Anthropocene begins in your town.

Holly Holmes

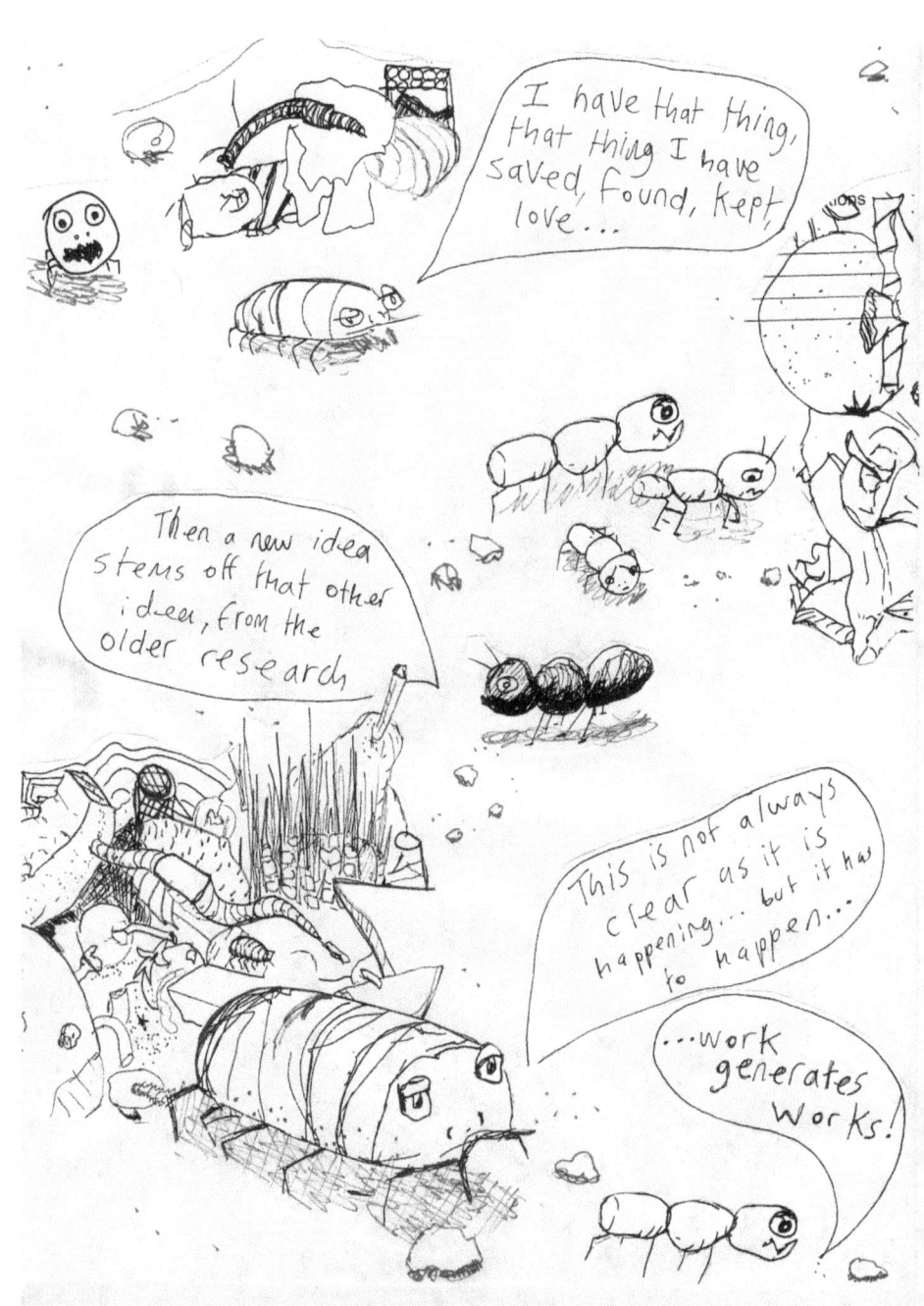

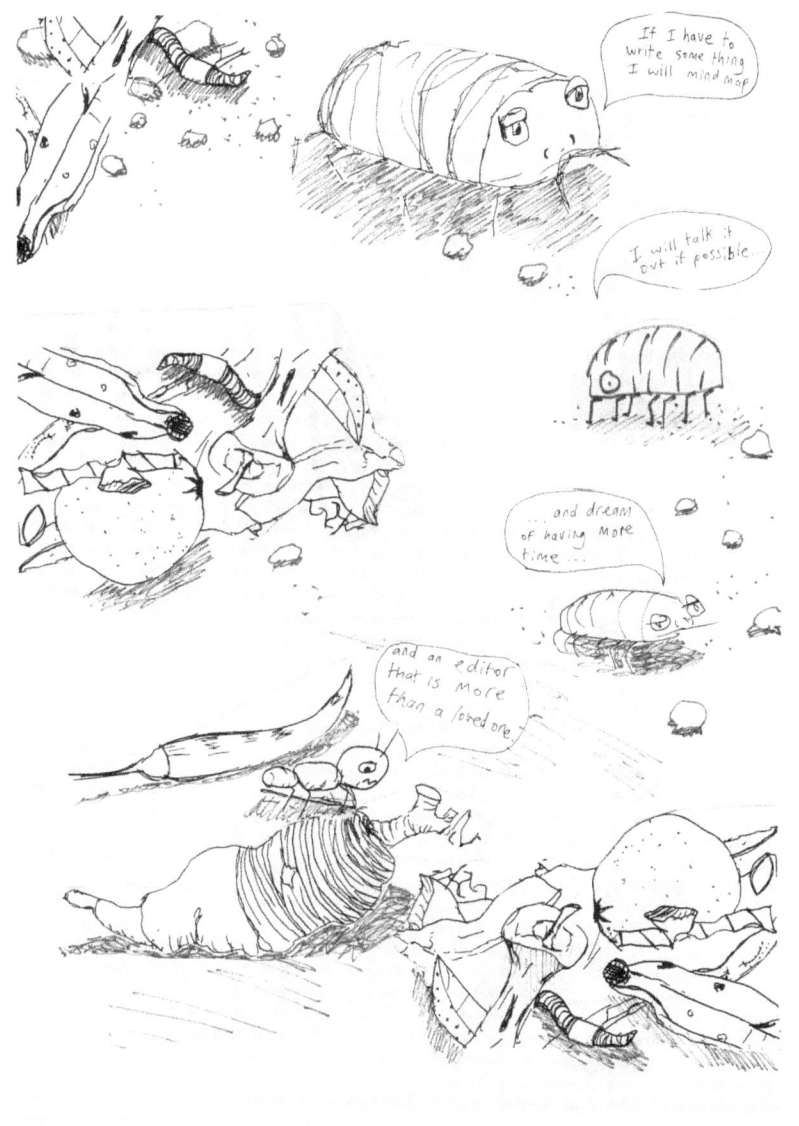

93

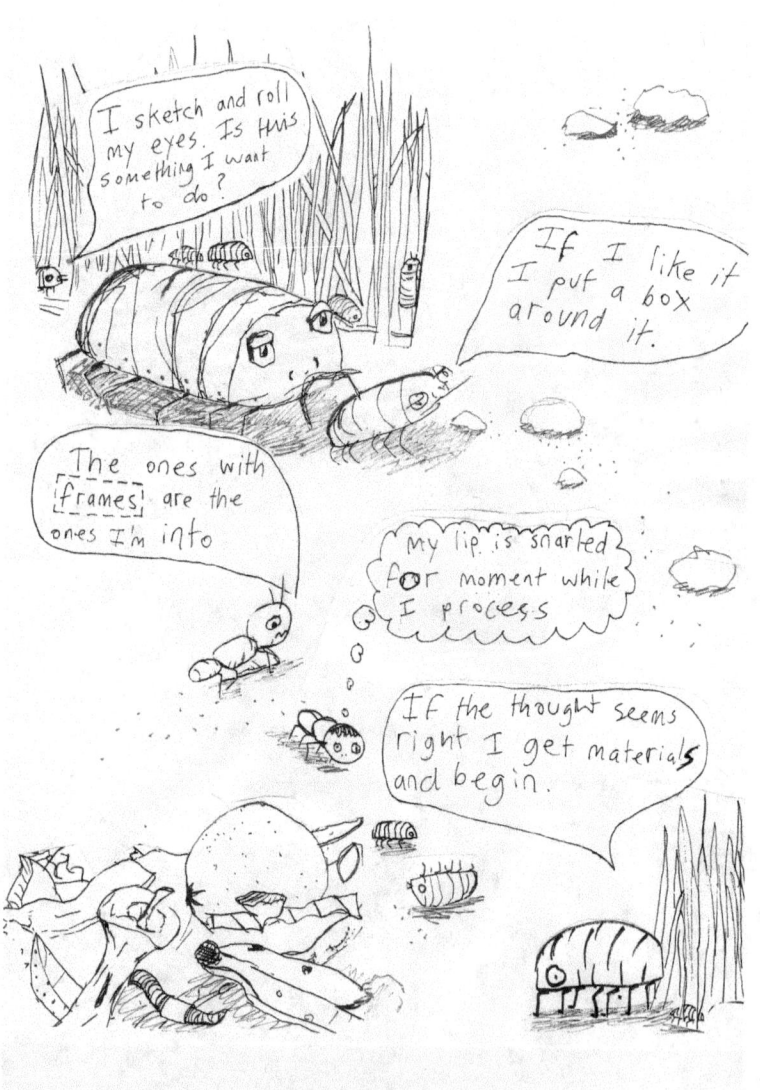

Regin Igloria

A LIST OF PEOPLE

Start with your family
then your other relatives
then your friends
people you work with
friends of friends
and maybe mild acquaintances
add people you've never met
but would like to

SEE YOU SOON!

Luke Joyner

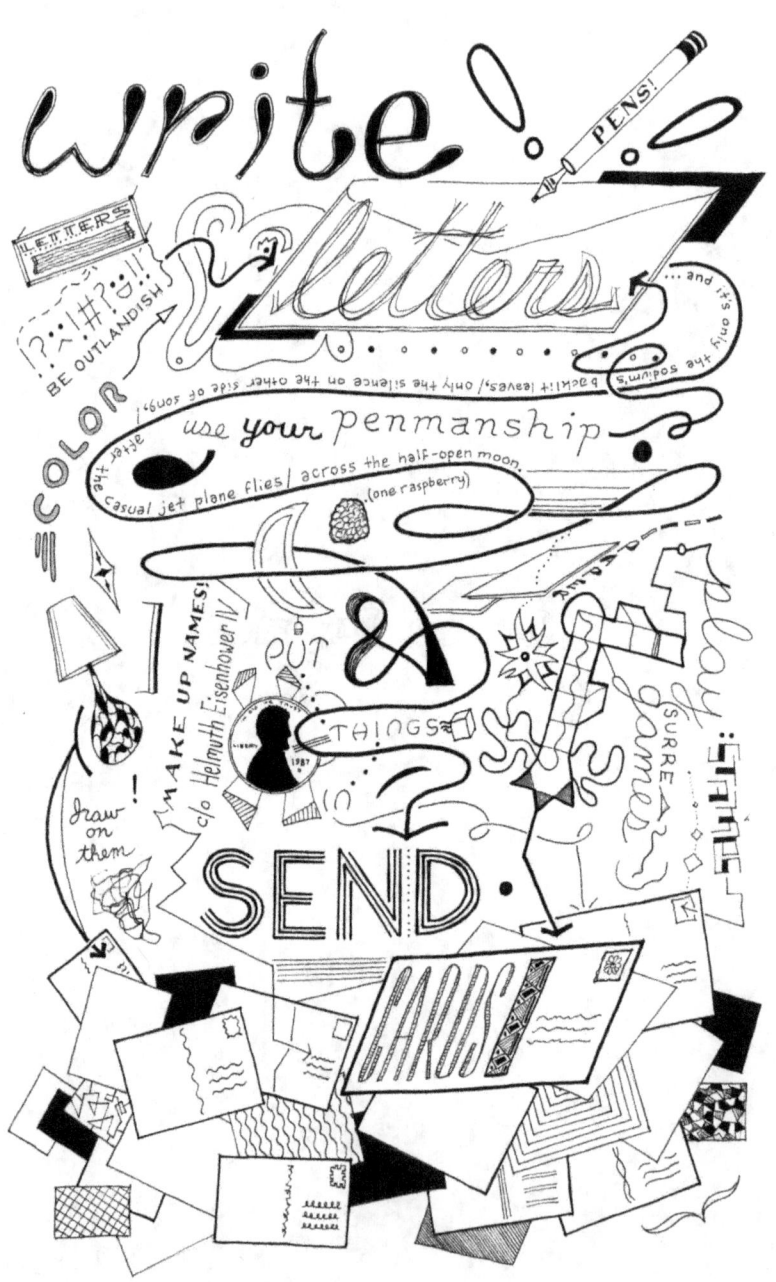

Luke Joyner says, "Send me something in the mail...
a poem, a drawing, rules and a first move for a play-
by-mail game, a dried leaf, anything. I'll send you
something back... My address is 1441 W Jarvis #3W,
Chicago, IL 60626"

Curtis Locke

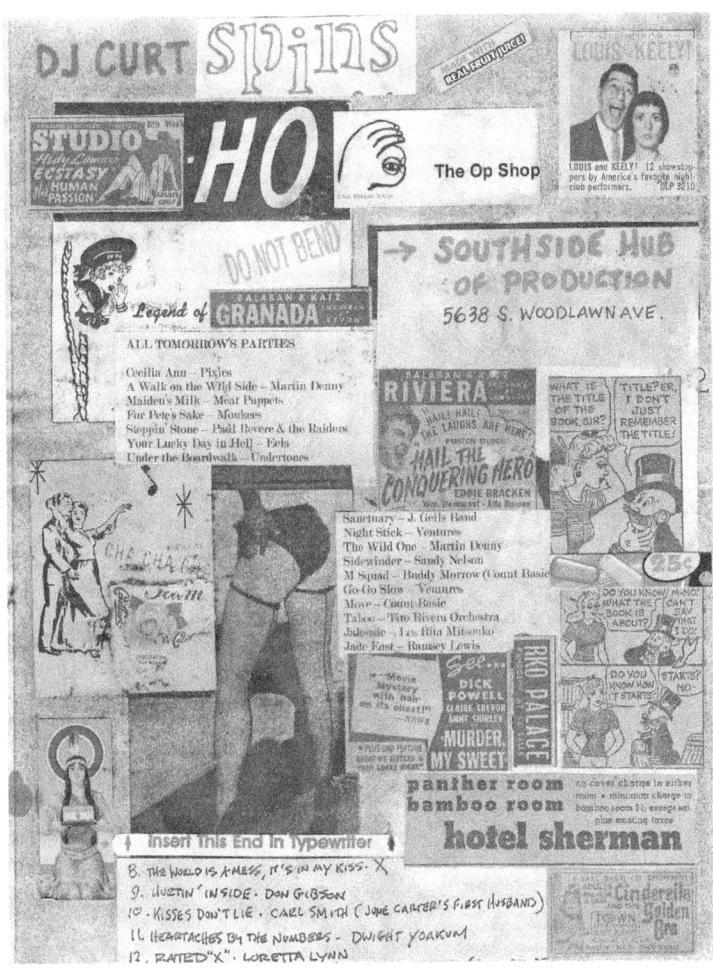

DJ CURT spins

STUDIO ECSTASY HUMAN PASSION

HO

The Op Shop

LOUIS ' KEELY!

LOUIS and KEELY! 12 showstoppers by America's favorite night club performers.

DO NOT BEND

Legend of GRANADA

→ SOUTHSIDE HUB OF PRODUCTION
5638 S. WOODLAWN AVE.

ALL TOMORROW'S PARTIES

Cecilia Ann – Pixies
A Walk on the Wild Side – Martin Denny
Maiden's Milk – Meat Puppets
For Pete's Sake – Monkees
Steppin' Stone – Paul Revere & the Raiders
Your Lucky Day in Hell – Eels
Under the Boardwalk – Undertones

RIVIERA
HAIL THE CONQUERING HERO
EDDIE BRACKEN

Sanctuary – J. Geils Band
Night Stick – Ventures
The Wild One – Martin Denny
Sidewinder – Sandy Nelson
M Squad – Buddy Morrow (Count Basie)
Go-Go Slow – Ventures
Move – Count Basie
Taboo – Tito Rivera Orchestra
Julousie – Les Hta Mitsanko
Jade East – Ramsey Lewis

DICK POWELL
MURDER, MY SWEET

RIO PALACE

panther room
bamboo room
hotel sherman

Insert This End in Typewriter

8. THE WORLD IS A MESS, IT'S IN MY KISS. X
9. HURTIN' INSIDE - DON GIBSON
10. KISSES DON'T LIE - CARL SMITH (JUNE CARTER'S FIRST HUSBAND)
11. HEARTACHES BY THE NUMBERS - DWIGHT YOAKUM
12. RATED "X". LORETTA LYNN

Cinderella Golden Era

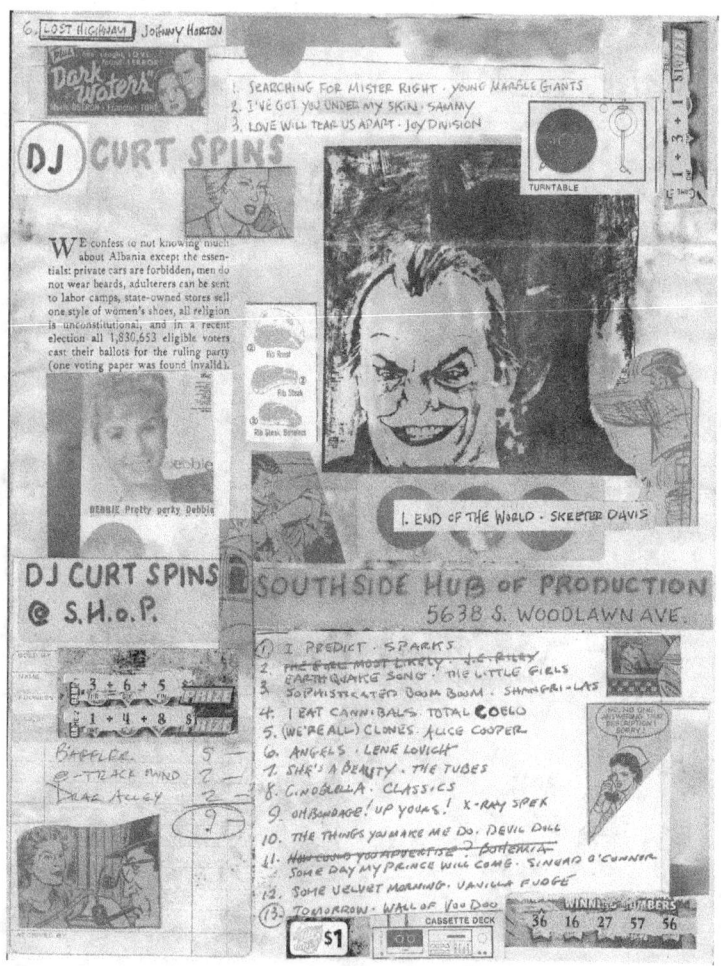

Flyers constructed with scissors, glue, vintage true crime comix, old theatre print ads from the 1940s , receipts, record sleeve album promos, food packaging graphics, discarded lotto tickets, mix-tape playlists, and self-cannibalized/recycled fliers embedded with black mold from basement storage water damage.

Gwenn-Aël Lynn

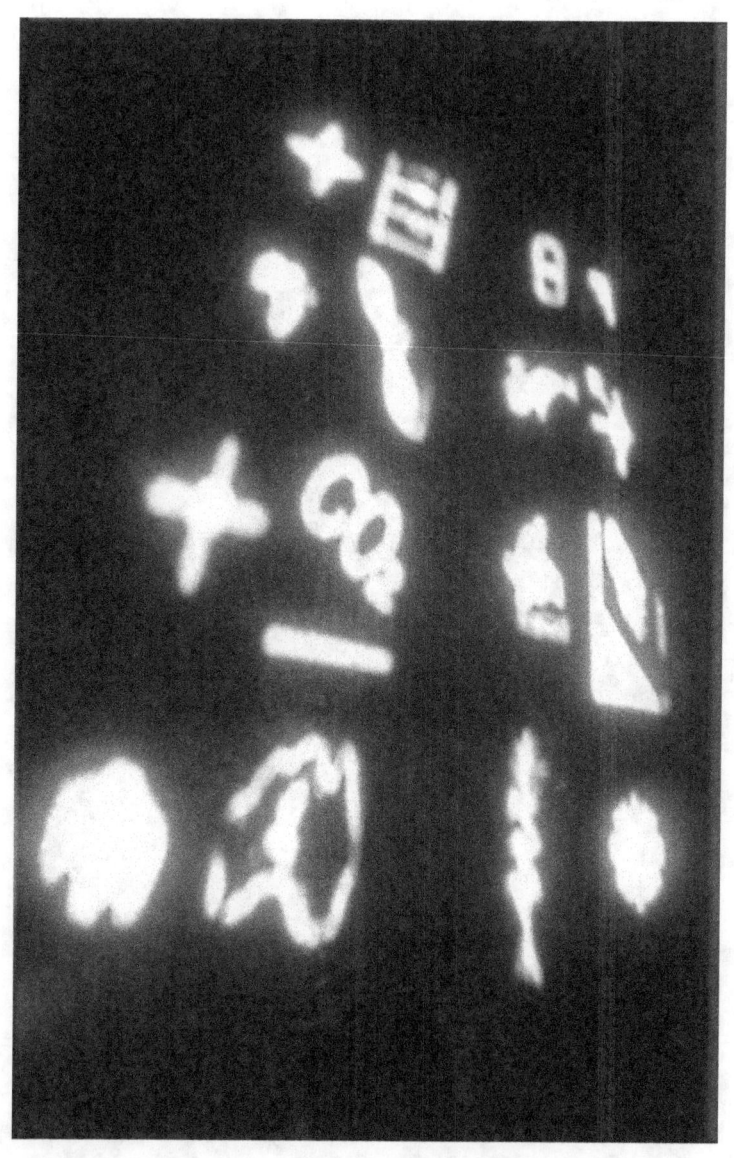

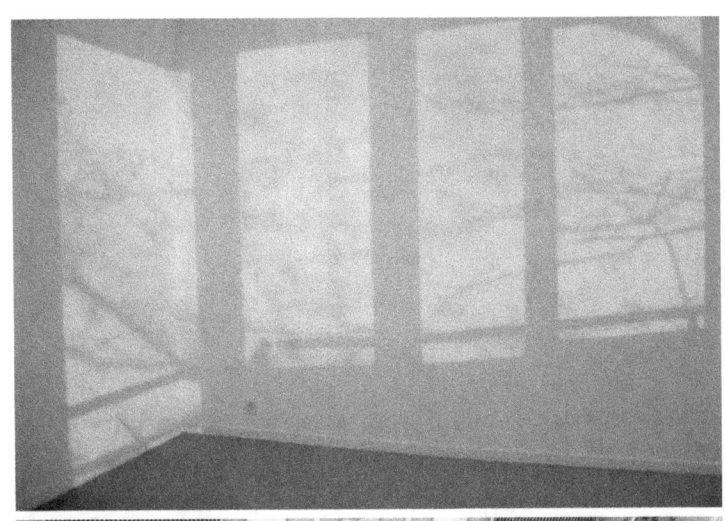

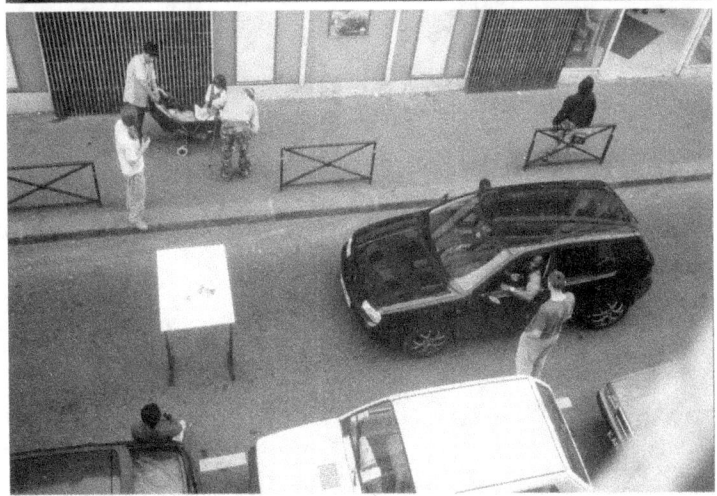

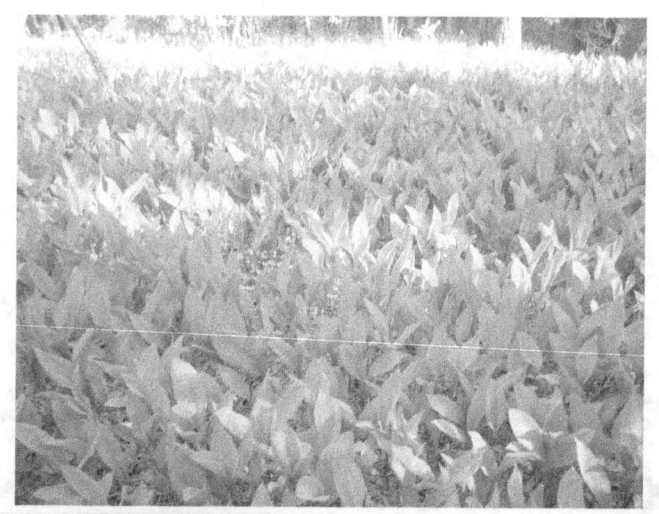

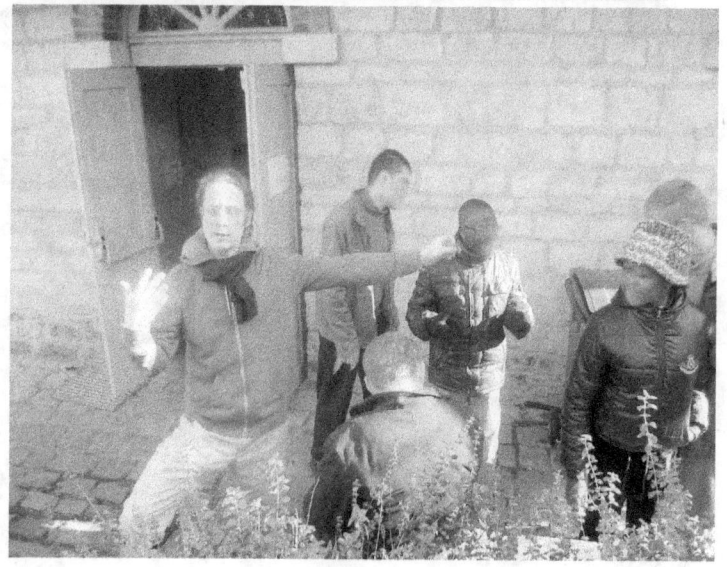

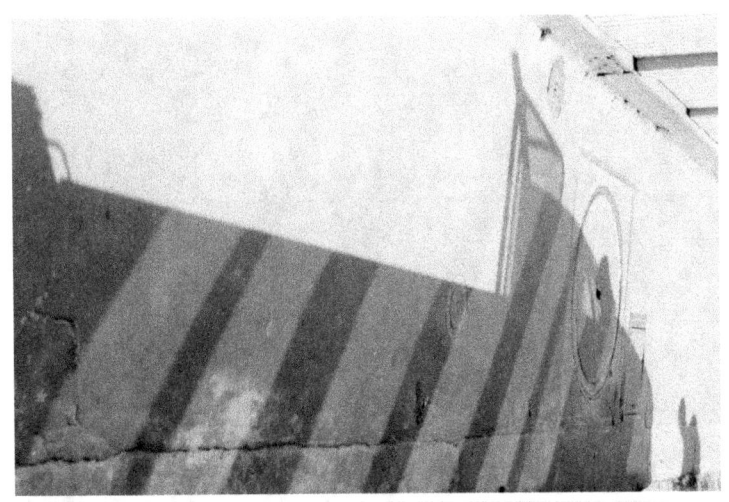

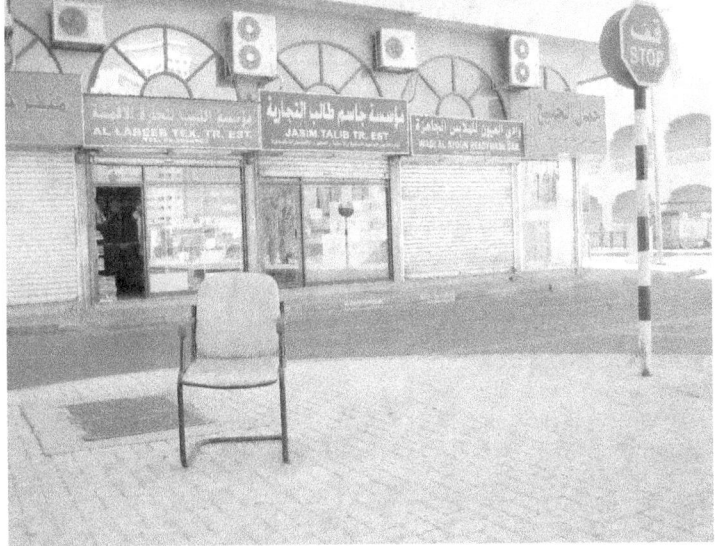

Mary King

Making Art.

I like to make rules. Here are some of mine:

Don't go out in the morning. Make art. Look at art.
Read about art. Think. Daydream.

Use the best room in your house or apartment for
making art.

If you need more room, use the kitchen.

Be brave. No idea is too dumb.

Work until you hit a wall. Then stop.

Spend a lot of time looking at what you have done.

If someone does something to offend you, make art
about it; but don't be mean. Use humor.

Look at real art in museums or galleries.

Instead of snapping photos, make little sketches of
what you see.

Attend your friends' exhibitions. Be supportive.

Form a group with other artists. Try to ask intelligent questions.

And finally, to feed your art, lead a complicated and fascinating life.

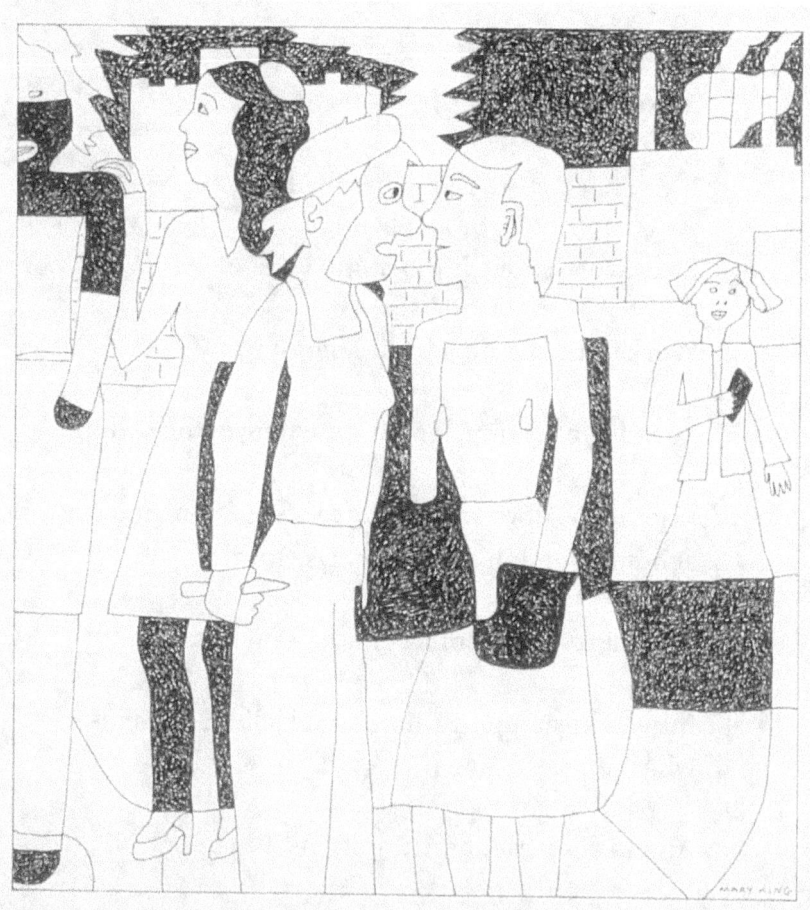

Hani Moustafa

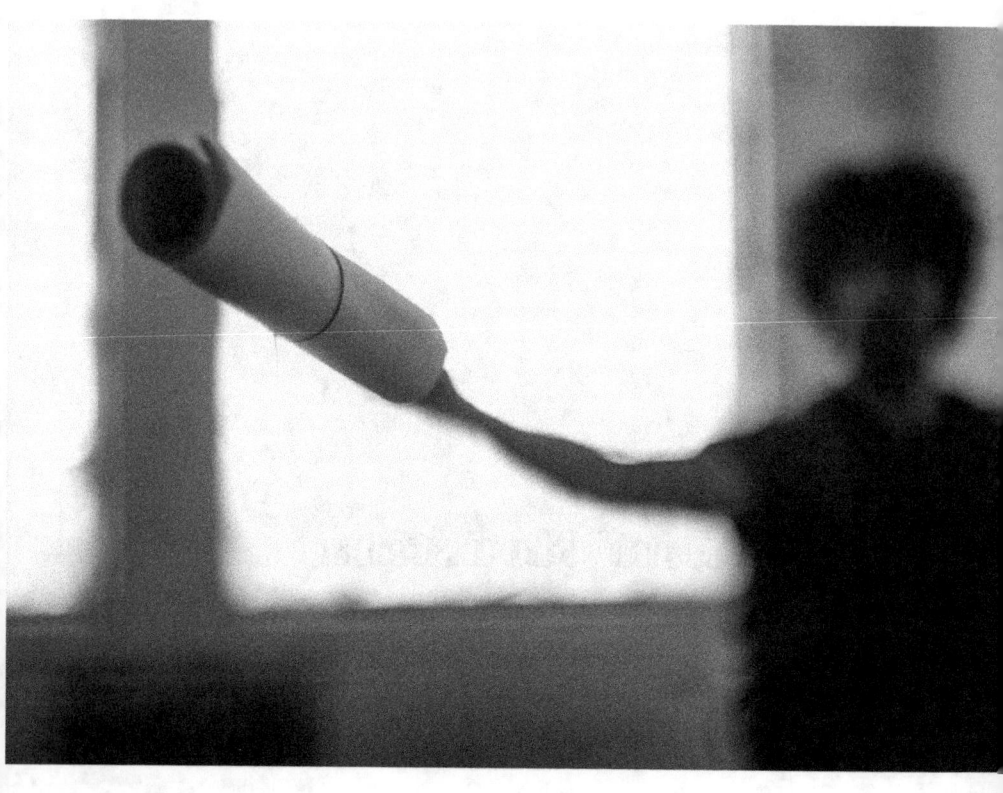

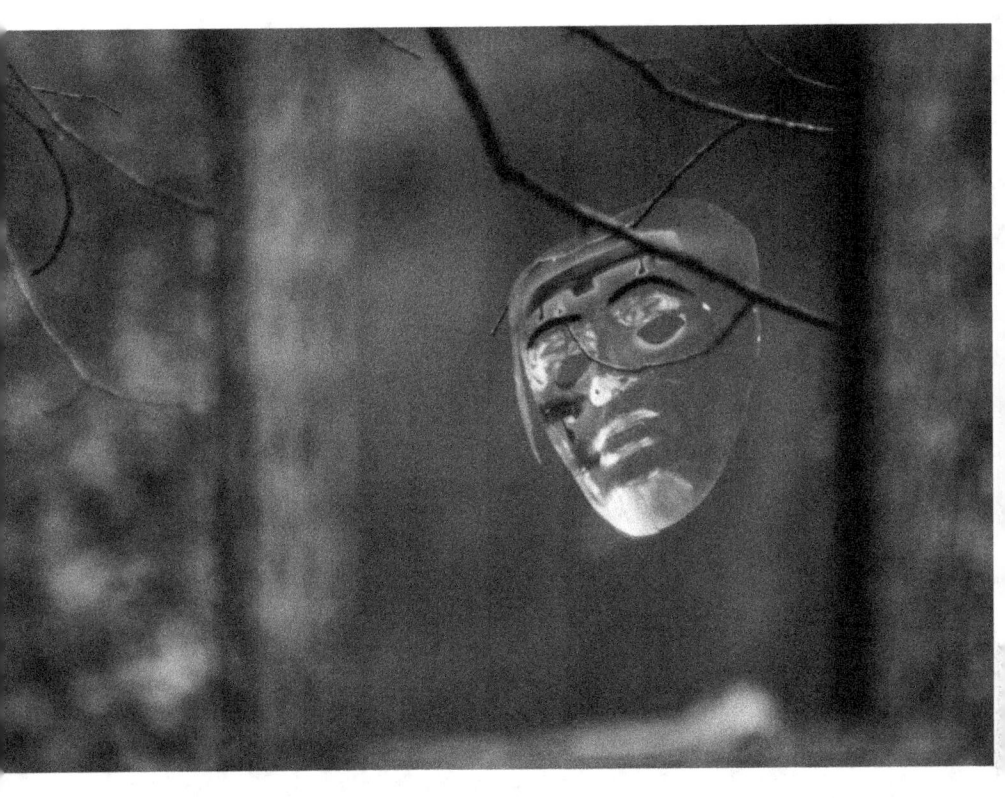

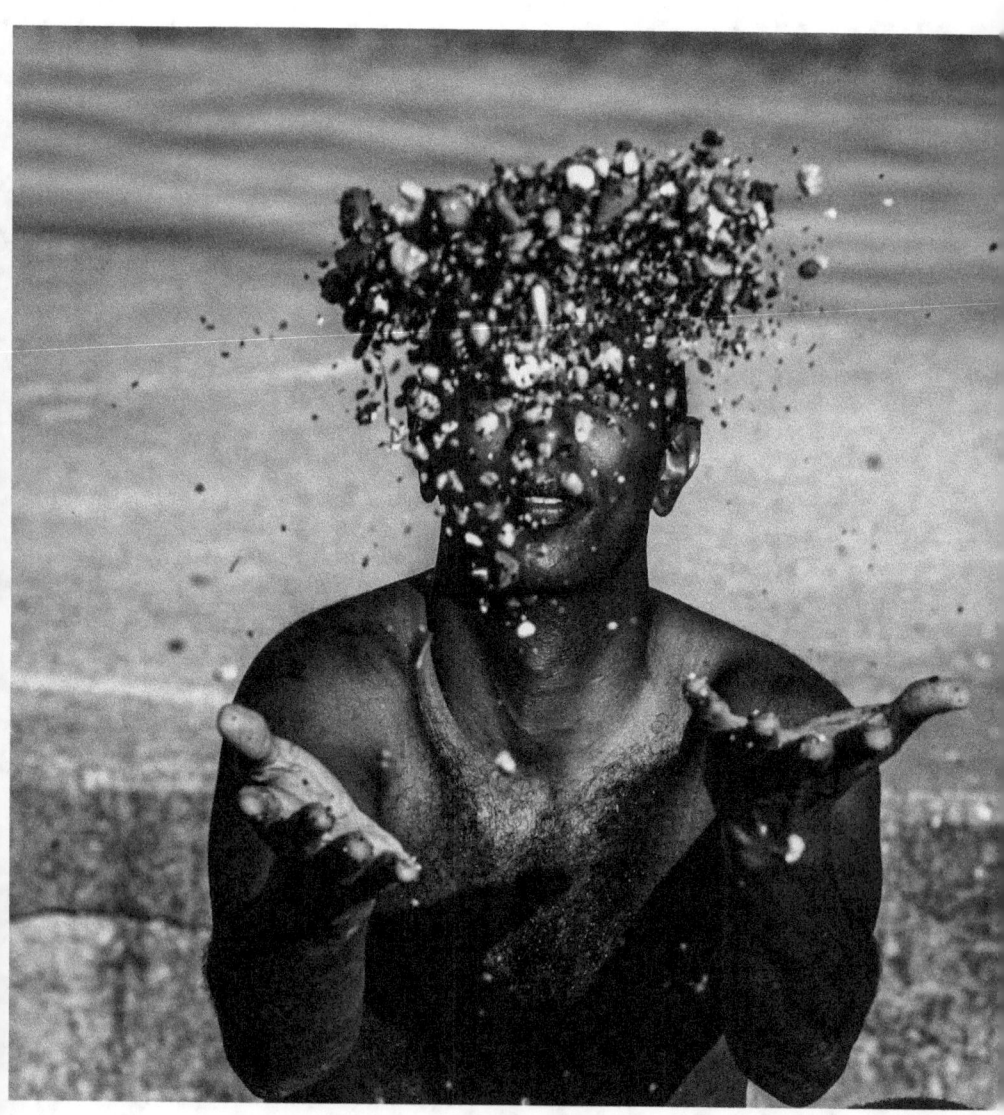

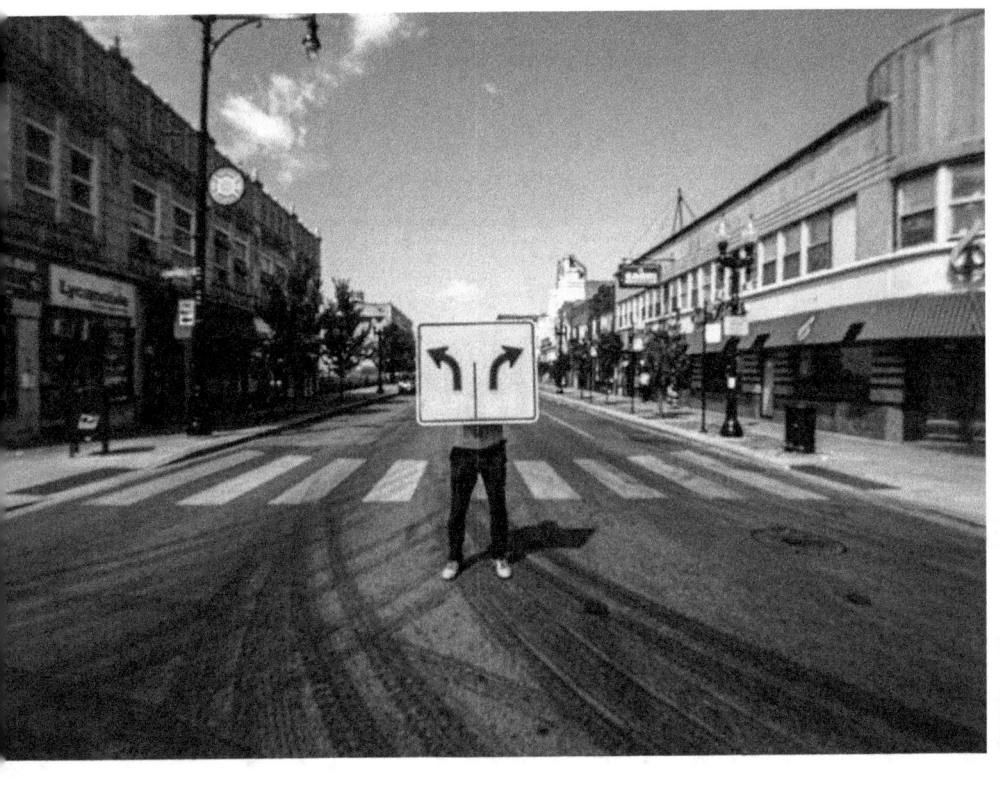

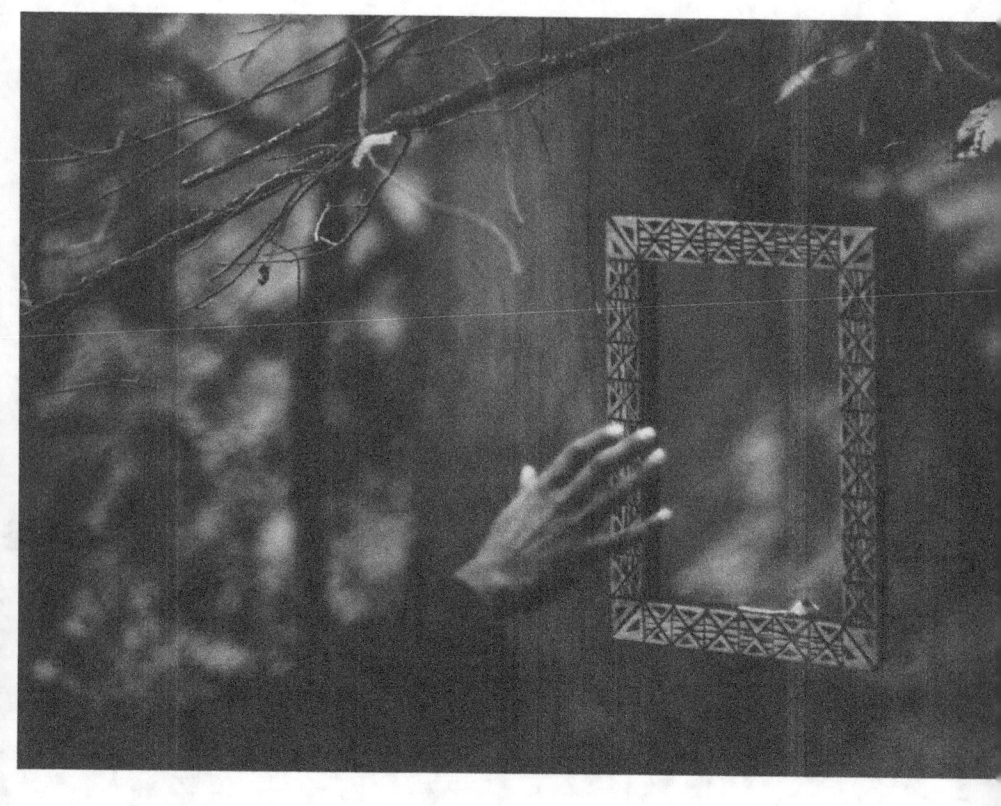

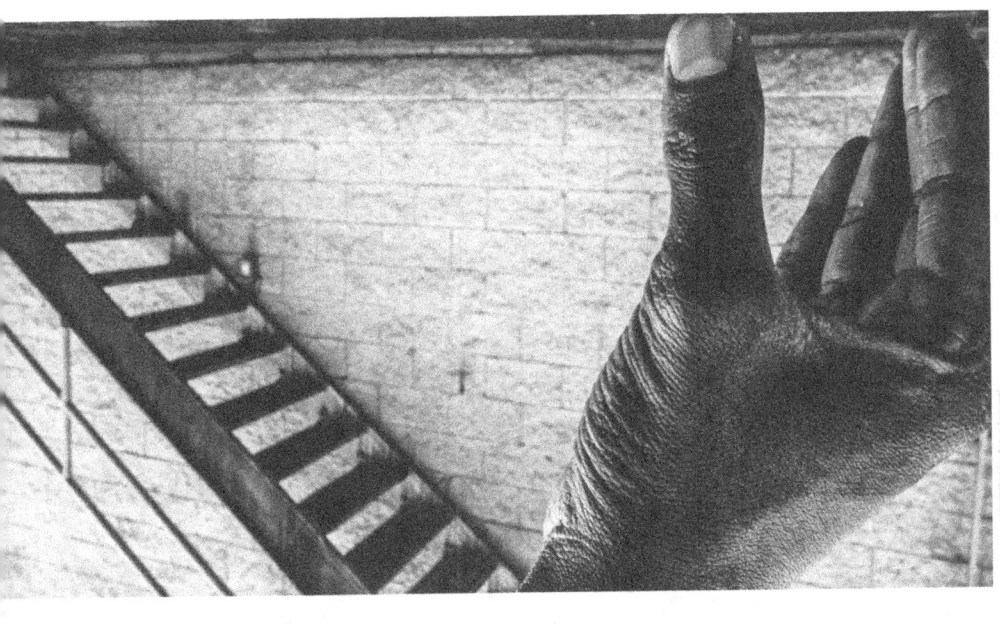

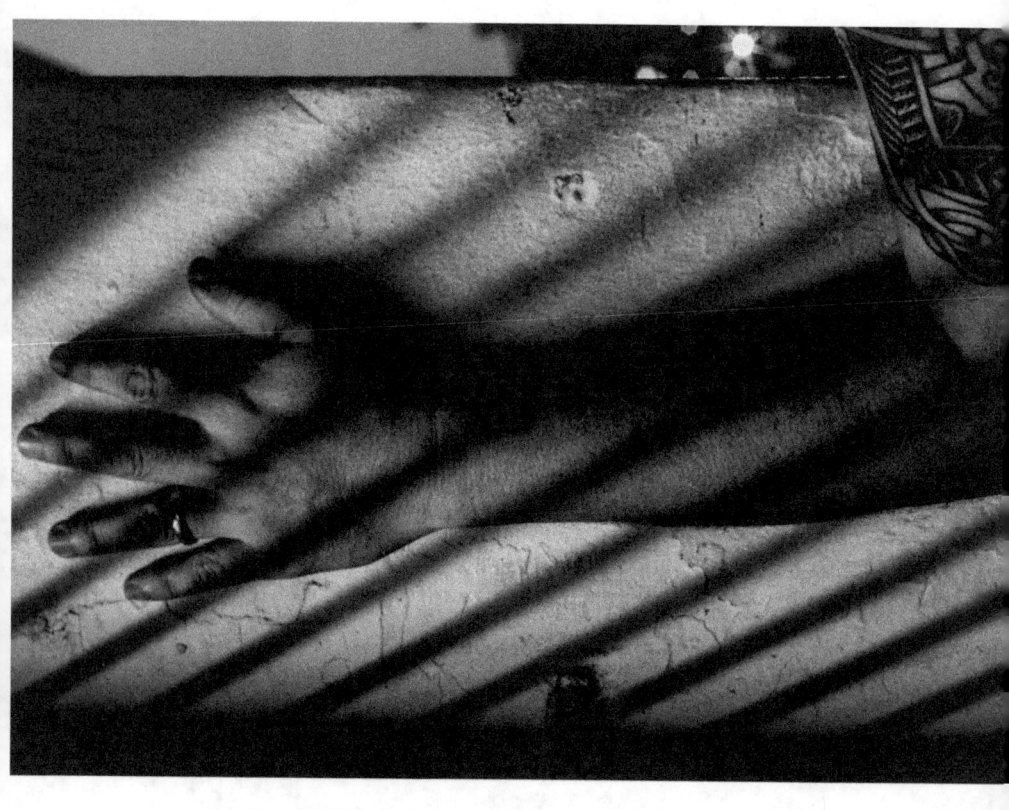

N55

We are all useful idiots!

THE POWER OF LOGIC VERSUS THE LOGIC OF POWER

It is quite simple: Either we learn how to share knowledge and resources in a fair way or we will destroy ourselves and the planet. Our current activities are totally ruining Earths biosphere. Environmental sustainability is only possible in a more just world where social sustainability is the core of the future societies.

To understand language on the most basic level and hereby logic and logical relations is probably our best chance to find new ways of living together in a better way that will enable us to leave a liveable planet for our children and future generations.

WE ARE ALL USEFUL IDIOTS!!!

Maybe understanding this sentence could lead to a new understanding of The Commons based on common stupidity?

The Commons
Open source
Peer to peer
Crowd Funding
Social Design
Urban Gardening
Sharing economy
Community coops
ecological food
creative commons

DIY strategies

etc etc etc

buzzwords

bla bla bla

The harsh reality is probably that none of all these
fantastic new ways of thinking and doing things (which
N55 are deeply involved in) are going to have any
substantial impact on our society until we understand the
following and implement it not only in our ways of thinking
but also in the way we treat each other, the way we
behave in all situations:

The following is not an expression of an opinion among
other equally important or unimportant opinions: Its based
on logical relations and facts. Its not an expression of an
ideology or the system of thoughts that one find in a
religion. Because subjective opinions, ideologies or
religions should never be used as the basis of political
statements or decisions. Politics must be based on logical
relations and facts. On whats right and whats wrong. Let
us look at a decisive logical relation, the relation between
persons and rights:

A person can be described in an infinite number of ways.
None of these descriptions can be completely adequate.
We therefore cannot describe precisely what a person is.
We do however have the possibility to point out necessary
relations between persons and other factors. We have to
respect these relations and factors in order not to
contradict ourselves and in order to be able to talk about
persons in a meaningful way. One necessary relation is
the relation between persons and bodies. It makes no

sense referring to a person without referring to a body. If we for example say: here we have a person, but he or she does not have a body, it does not make sense. Furthermore, there are necessary relations between persons and the rights of persons. Persons should be treated as persons and therefore as having rights. If we deny this assertion it goes wrong: here is a person, but this person should not be treated as a person, or: here is a person, who should be treated as a person, but not as having rights. Therefore we can only talk about persons in a way that makes sense if we know that persons have rights.

This leads to understanding politics on the most basic level:

The fundamental purpose of politics is to protect the rights of persons. If we deny this assertion we get: the fundamental purpose of politics is not to protect the rights of persons. This suggests that one of the basic tasks of politicians could be, for example, to renounce the rights of themselves and of others. This has no meaning. Or that there is a more important purpose to politics which does not have anything to do with persons and therefore also has nothing to do with the rights of persons. That is plain nonsense. Therefore, we now know that the basic purpose of politics is to protect the rights of persons. In other words we can not talk about politics in a way that makes sense without the assumption that the fundamental purpose of politics is to protect the rights of persons.

Our current most devastating political problem is the following:

Concentrations of power characterise our society. Concentrations of power do not always respect the rights of persons. If one denies this fact one gets:

concentrations of power always respect the rights of persons. This does not correspond with our experiences. Concentrations of power force persons to concentrate on participating in competition and power games, in order to create a social position for themselves. Concurrently with the concentrations of power dominating our conscious mind and being decisive to our situations, the significance of our fellow humans diminishes. And our own significance becomes the significance we have for concentrations of power, the growth of concentrations of power, and the conflicts of concentrations of power.
It is clear that persons should be consciously aware of the rights of persons and therefore must seek to organise the smallest concentrations of power possible. Its clear that we have to find ways of living with as small concentration of power as possible.

How can we imagine that this situation could be changed?

We call our societies democratic despite the fact that our cities are monuments of injustice and unfairness. Capital and the institutional forces behind it rules. Large concentrations of power make the decisions that shape our behaviour and our lives in general. Our cities act as parasites on the planets resources and environment. The exploitation is staged and controlled by large concentrations of power.

We are all useful idiots.

If we don't take this serious we will probably end up destroying not only ourselves but also the planet that we want our children to inherit.

in order to survive we most likely have to learn how to distribute power and resources in a fair and rational way, produce locally, learn how to share and collaborate instead of competing, to break down hierarchies and to find ways of existing with as small concentrations of power as possible.

One may argue that phenomena like open source potentially could have a big impact on our society. That it will empower people. But its most likely not enough to produce decisive change. Banks, churches, super wealthy individuals, corrupted administrations, states and multinational cooperate structures have immense power. If Open Source really becomes influential, concentrations of power will find ways of controlling it.

Maybe there is hope in the current uprisings erupting simultaneously around the world ? Maybe we need a reinvention of violent activism? Maybe the middle class will react in new surprising and potentially revolutionary ways? Maybe we simply need to learn how to share for real?

Even well-meaning people with good intentions are tempted to work for the concentrations of power that they ought to do away with. Most architects, urban planners, designers, artists etc are more than willing to work for these concentrations of power despite the fact that these concentrations of power do not necessarily respect the rights of persons. Even alternative strategies in arts, design, architecture etc ends up becoming absorbed by concentrations of power.

Maybe we have a fantastic chance to create a better world if we acknowledge the fact that a large part of the people living in the current societies in the western world in reality don't have a job. Maybe the better world is already there? The fact is that a vast number of people are kept alive and fed by the states and at the same time told that they are unworthy and should be ashamed. Even without a redistribution of resources and power, societies are already sustaining lives of people that don't have to work. And most likely will never work. And more and more people will be out of work when robots take over the hard labor in the industry as well as jobs that requires longer educations like the jobs of lawyers and doctors. Not just in the west but also in China etc. Why don't we accept that fact and distribute power and resources. This would allow people to spend their time learning, researching, designing houses that lasts and produce more energy than they consume, discussing, being nice to each other, playing, etc?

Why don't we set people free and create a positive identity of being a good productive citizen without a job? Why don't we set a limit to how rich one can get and redistribute resources in a fair way?

The Greeks discovered logic and democracy 2000 years ago. Their wealth was based on two things: Silver mines and slaves. We have plenty of silver and other resources if we learn to distribute it better and find ways of existing with as small concentrations of power as possible.

Let us enslave the robots before they enslave us and learn to be free and be nice to each other.

Let us create a better world!

N55

Justin Nalley

Anders Nilsen

COMICS LOOP

This is a collaborative comics game that should result in maximum hilarity, creativity, unexpectedness and delight. The set-up is a little involved but it's actually just as much fun as the comic-drawing part.

SET UP

Get between one and twenty friends together who can draw okay or at least are willing to try.

Get sixty 3 x 5 cards, or tear some printer paper into sixty little pieces.

On twenty of them: write a simple **character** description on each card in **one or two words** (pregnant teenager, drunk person, the devil, et.).

On twenty others write a simple description of an **object** (magnifying glass, flashlight, etc... again one or two words, max).

On twenty others write a one or two word description of a **setting** (vacant house, puddle etc).

Each participant is randomly given one **character** card, one **object** card, and one **setting** card.

Now everyone should get **five new small pieces of paper**... like, say, a piece of printer paper torn into four or six evenly sized pieces.

Everyone has **two minutes** (someone will have to keep time) to draw the character they got, being instructed **not** to draw them in a stereotypical way, or in a way they have seen before. Repeat this step **two more times**, being sure to draw your character in a **totally different way each time**.

Everyone has **two more minutes** to draw their **object**, two more minutes to draw their **setting**.

All of the drawings get pinned or taped to a wall.

Everyone votes for their favorites: Everyone has **three votes** to allocate to their favorite character(s) by making a small hatch mark or check in the lower left corner of the drawing. You can assign your hatch marks to three different characters or two to one and one to another or whatever. However you want.

Everyone has three votes for their favorite **object(s)** and for the **setting(s)** as well.

The top **three** vote-getting characters are selected (in the event of a tie you may ask some non-participant to come vote as well, or discuss among you). The top **two** Objects and the top **two** Settings are selected as well (if you have a lot of people you might want to include an extra object and/or setting). Put these winning cards together on the wall where everyone can consult them for reference.

MAKING THE COMIC

Now everyone gets a piece of paper. 8 1/2 x 11 printer paper is fine. Divide it into six roughly even square panels.

Everyone vote on whether you want this to be a **silent comic** or whether **dialogue** between characters is allowed. I would actually recommend silent the first time you try this. And if not everyone in the group is fluent in the same language a silent comic is a good way to go, too.

In the lower right (last) panel of the page everyone has three minutes **(or four or five depending on how serious you want to be)** to **draw a picture** involving at least one of the characters, one of the objects and one of the settings. **The character should be doing something,** or something should apparently **just have happened** or be **about to happen**. No boring "just standing around" drawings allowed.

Once that panel is done everyone passes their paper to the person on their **left**.

On your new piece of paper: in the **top left panel** you will now take 3-5 minutes to draw a new panel **FOLLOWING** the one you just drew on the other page. That is: when you're done you will have created a two-panel comic strip that **starts on the bottom of one page** and **continues on the top of the next one**. Yes, this is un-intuitive. Just go with it.

Now lay out all the pages in order on a table so everyone can look at them.

Each page should now have a **first** and **last** panel on it. At this stage it's a good idea to try and come to a consensus as to which page (which **first panel**) might make a good first panel for a longer story... keeping in mind that the panel that 'precedes' it will therefore become the 'end' of the story. **Number the pages** to help everyone keep them straight as you all work.

Everyone's next job will be to **connect** the two unrelated panels on someone else's paper by drawing the **rest of the story** in the four panels in **between** them.

SO

Devise a system to determine an order for people to proceed (first, second, third, etc) to choose which page to finish. This could be alphabetical, or by drawing numbers out of a hat, or whatever.

The **first person** chooses the page they want to use and takes it, second person chooses from the remaining pages, etc. As everyone picks up the page they want to finish the only rule is you can't choose a page you've already drawn on. If people want to **trade**, they can.

At this stage it can be fun and useful to discuss a bit between yourselves what you want to do in order to create continuity... or not depending on how much you like randomness.

Now each person draws in the **missing four panels** to connect the first and last panels that already exist on their paper. You can use as many or as few of the Characters, Objects and Settings as you wish. try and make it make as much sense as is possible. And try and respect the two existing panels on your page and use them as your guide. You can set a time limit (3-5 minutes) or not as you wish.

When everyone is done, lay the pages out on a table again, or tape them up on the wall and look at them together. What do you see? Did themes emerge? Did people use the various elements in similar or radically different ways? **Does the 'story' make 'sense'?** Did the objects transform? Did the characters transform? How? Why?

Frederick Nitsch

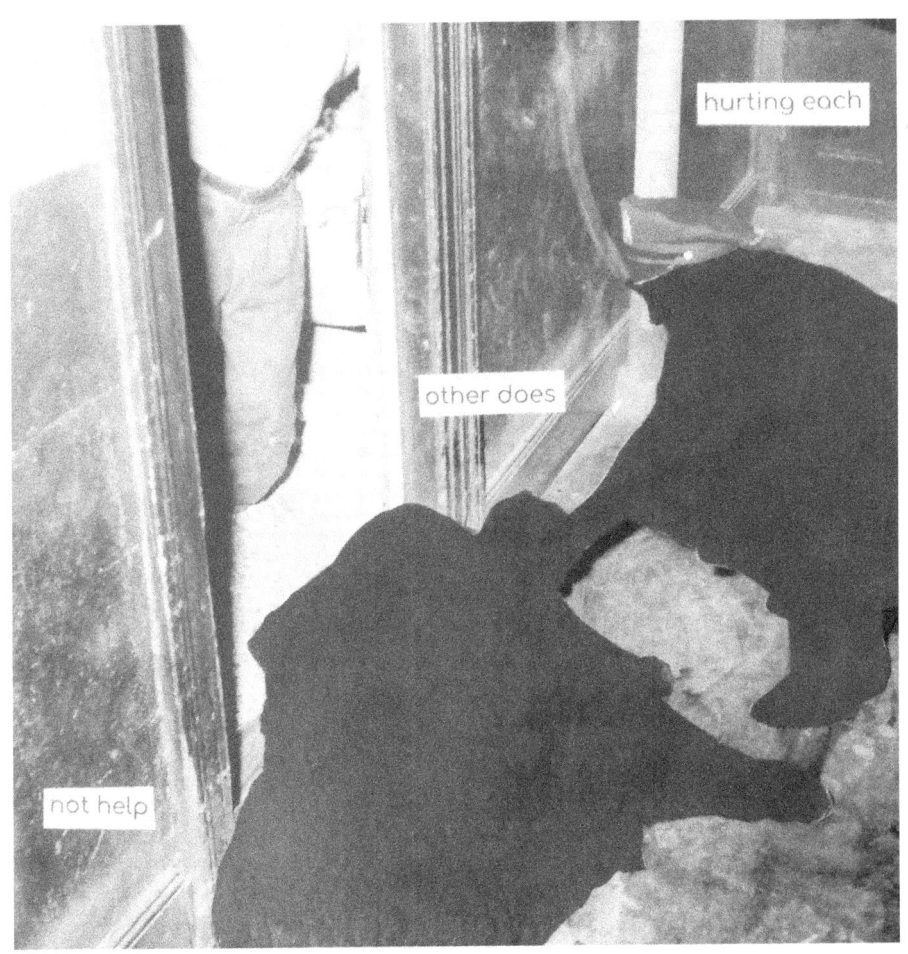

135

Andrew Nord

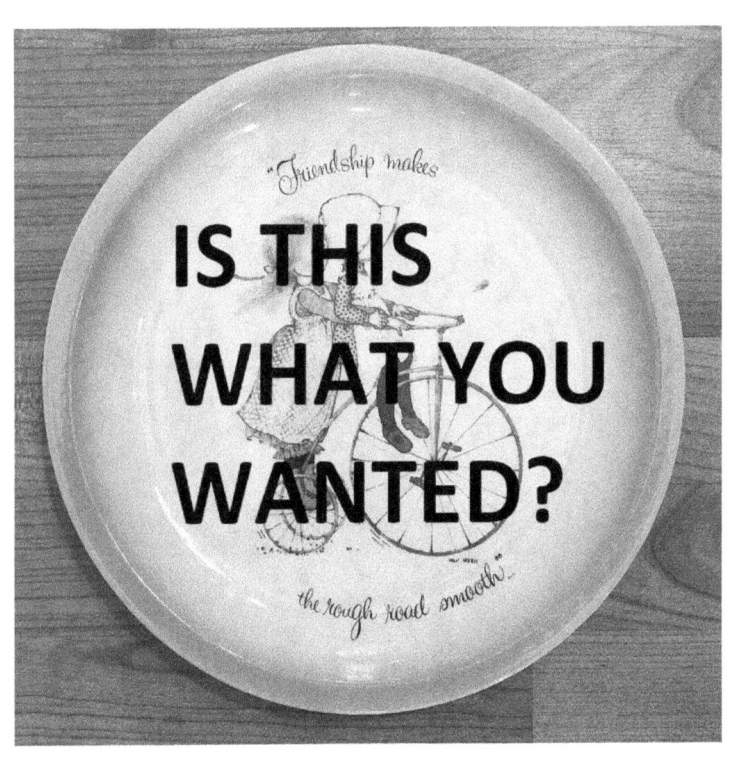

Jasper Nord

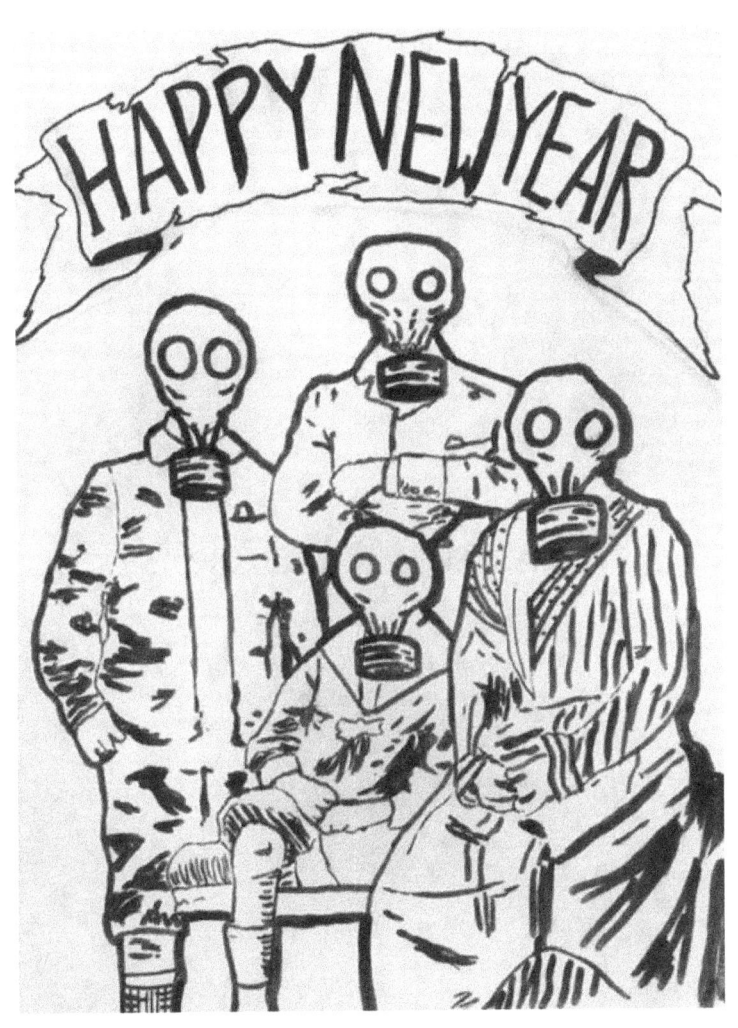

Teresa Pankratz

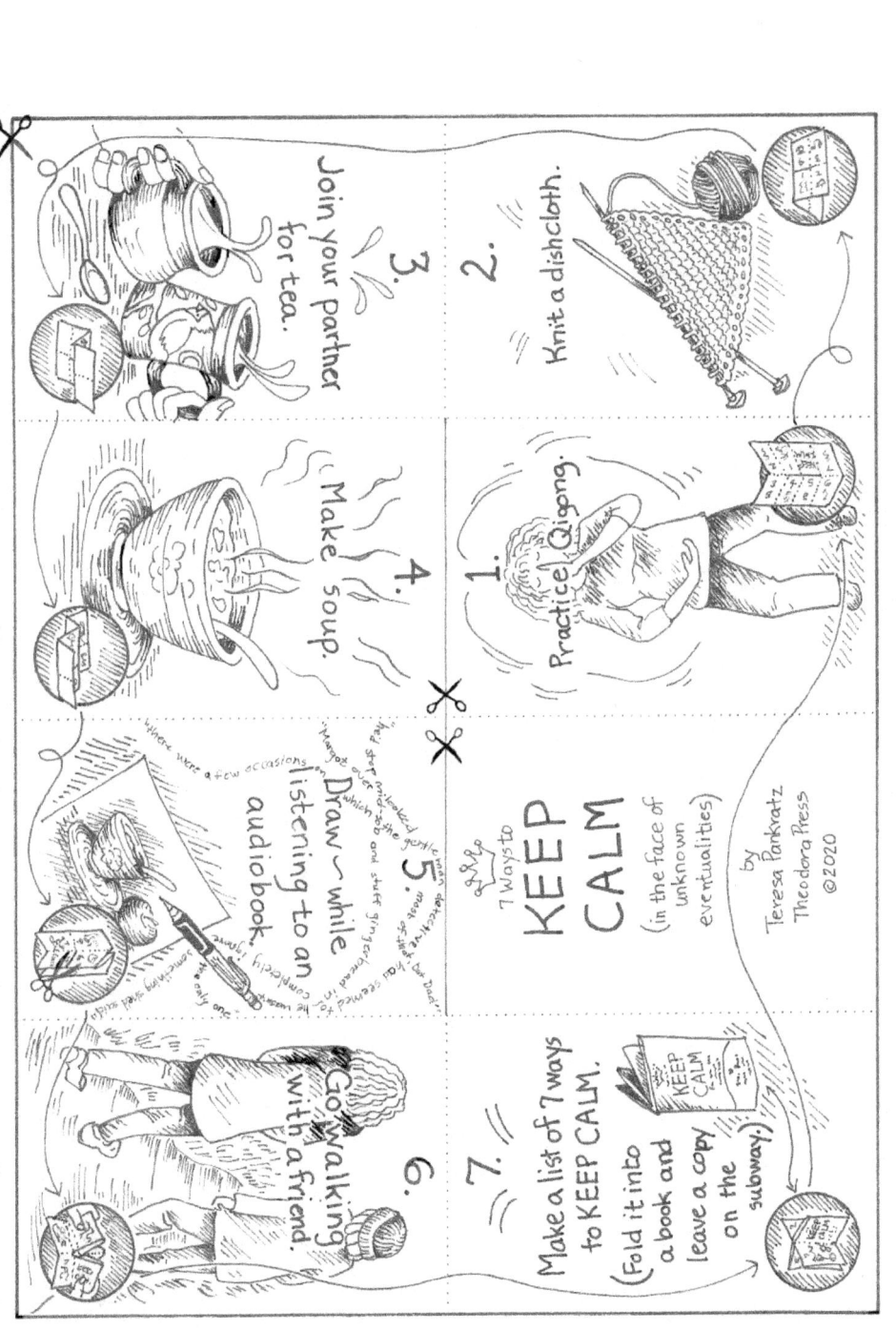

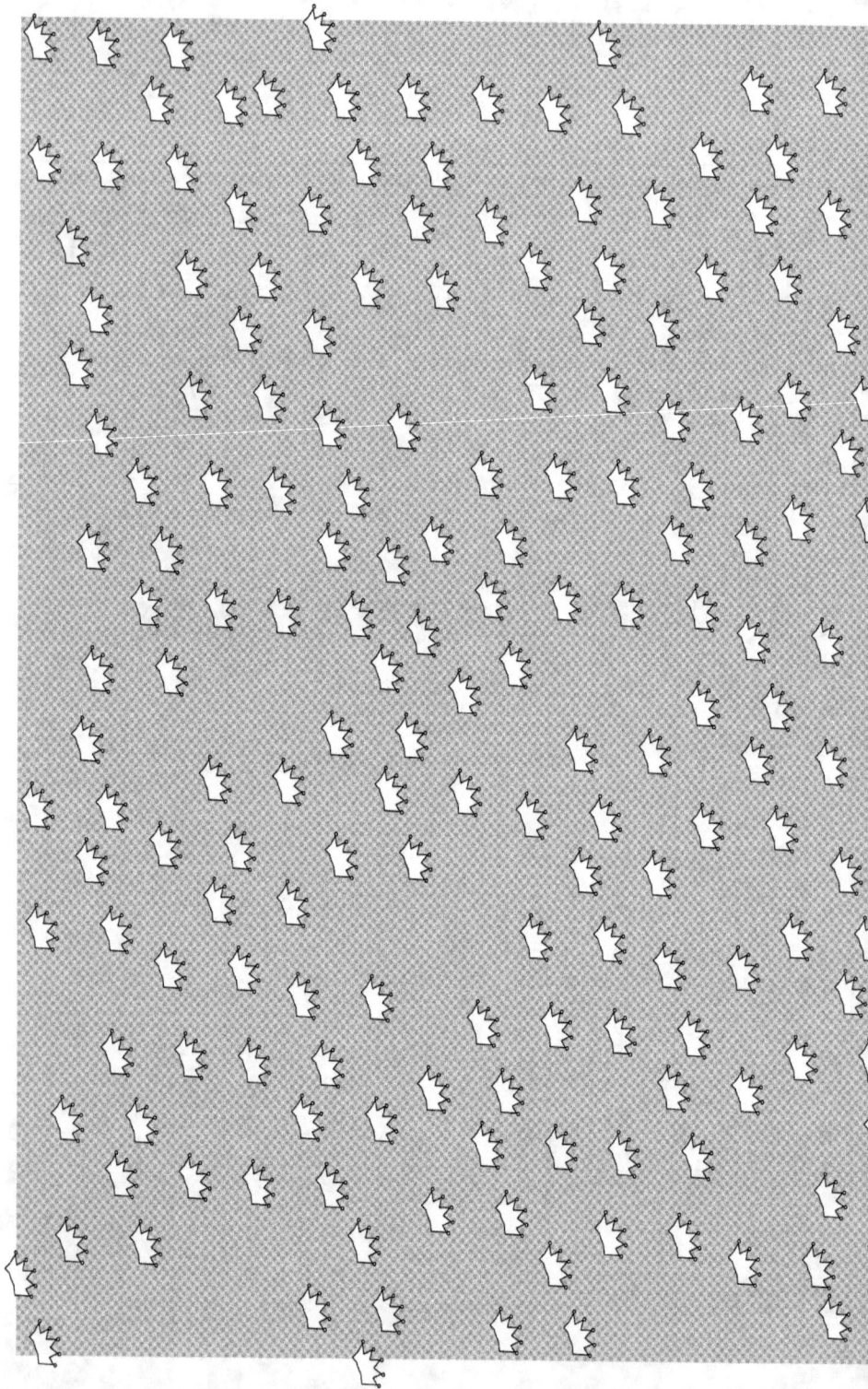

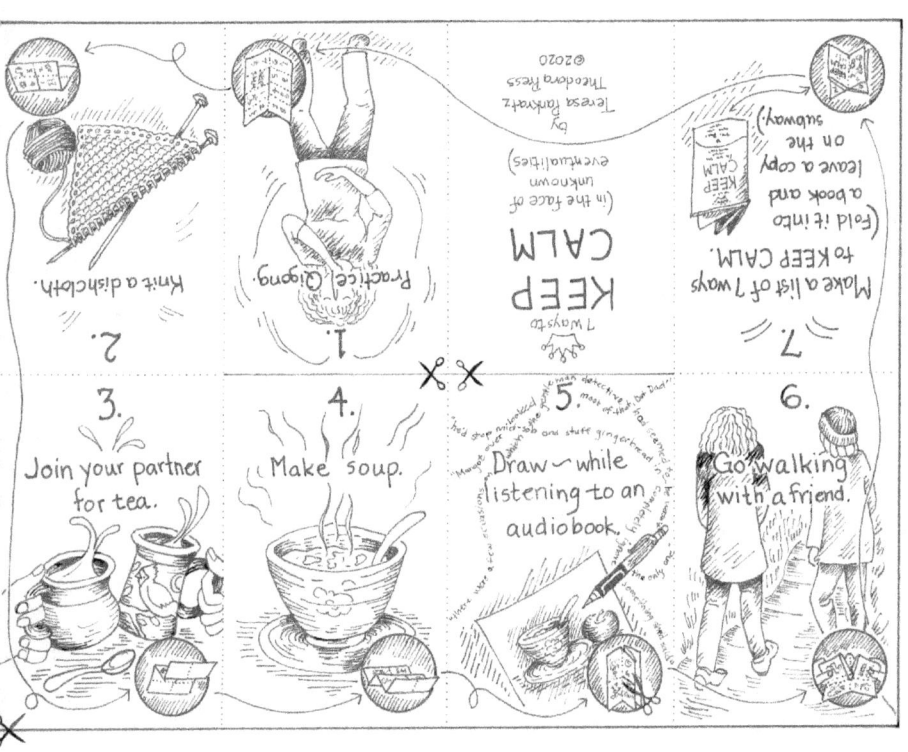

The image on this page can be kept in this book; the one on page 141 can be cut out and turned into a booklet which can then be stored anywhere in this book.

Andrew Gryf Paterson

Not knowing something (as a good start for a workshop)

This creative-proposal writing workshop involves guiding participants through a reflective and projective methodology for creative action and planning, beginning with the position of 'not knowing something' and wishing to learn more about it.

Each step of the exercise process aims to elaborate upon what one wishes to learn; who knows about it; what activities may be generated by this urge; and who would be good company to do it with.

Different activites are imagined individually, considering the 'what, when, where, how' questions, as well as considering support for the action and maybe funding sources.

Afterwards thoughts emerging from the process are shared, including details as desired. Learning together may be crucial, and common minds found.

You could argue this process is a common tool for project planning. Hopefully you have asked some of these questions to yourself or others before.

The method of starting from 'not knowing something' has been successfully applied in the inter/trans-disciplinary cultural productions called 'Alternative Economy

Cultures' and 'Herbologies/ Foraging
Networks' programmes, with were shared in
Pixelache Helsinki Festival 2009 & 2010
respectively, ISEA2010 Ruhr, and other
local cultural forums.

This 'Not Knowing Something' exercise
first took took place as a workshop on a
sunny terrace at the Inter-format
Symposium at Nida Art Colony, Lithuania,
4-6.5.2011
[http://nidacolony.lt/en/news/78-inter-
format-symposium]. It is presented again
as a remote workshop contribution to
'Workshopology' Symposium of KIBLIX 2011
Festival in Maribor, Slovenia, 19-
20.11.2011
[http://www.kiblix.org/kiblix11/?en/sympos
ium.html].

Gratitude to those who take part in the
exercise and discussion, contributing to
its development in our minds.

Link: https://archive.org/details/agryfp-
2011-not-knowing-something

Published under a Peer Production license:
http://p2pfoundation.net/Peer_Production_L
icense
Attribution: Andrew Gryf Paterson,
http://agryfp.info

.

Notes from 1st workshop session at Inter-
Format Symposium, Nida Art Colony:

Involve others in knowledge development,
We try our best, It will be messy,
Openness, It is impossible to plan
everything, Idea-survival, Setting
frameworks for involvement, Person can
choose how to engage, Selecting out what
is interesting from a field (of science),
How to open up 'this is my idea, how can
you contribute?'

Notes from 2nd workshop session at
Workshopology Symposium, KIBLIX Festival:
Not-yet-become

....

.

Exercise

+++ What are the goals:

* To imagine new trans/inter/un-
disciplinary activities
* To share strategies for project design
based on not-being-expert
* To cross reference other people's ideas
for new collaborations
* To gain some experience in creative
proposal writing exercises

+++ Social matrix:

* eg. Individual work, collective
discussion

+++ Timespan:

60 mins minimum

+++ Preparation

* None needed except paper/notebook &
writing/typing tool

+++ Introduction (5 mins)

* This will be a step by step creative
proposal writing exercise, which are
similar to creative writing prompt
exercises where the workshop lead guides
you through steps individually, but in the
company of others, towards at least a
prototype version of a new creative
endeavour (such as a poem or short story).
In this case it will hopefully new
trans/inter/un- disciplinary cultural
activity with others.

+++ Activity (30 mins)

This part is read out/audio files played
as prompts to the workshop participants..

Think about what you would like to
learn something that you currently know
nothing about that could become your next
project (maybe consider it 'creative
research')..

Now What
What is the activity that relates to
this thing that you don't know?
What is motivating you to try to learn
about it?

Are you ready to take on the burden now
to do the activity?

Now Who
Who inspires/inspired you to do it? /
Who are the people doing this activity
that you know?
Who might be people who are doing
something similar? (for example in another
field/discipline/occupation)

Now Where
How might it relate to the where you
live or where you come from?
Where might you find other people who
are doing this activity?
Where might be good places to do it?

Now When
When does this activity happen?
(Context, Nature-, Social-)

It is impossible to plan everything..

.

Past What
What was done in the past?
What are the historical connections of
this activity?
What has changed since?

Future What
What is possible to do?
What formats?
What processes?
What events?
Within what field/discipline/?

Future Who
Who might be interested to get involved
or take part? (groups or individuals)
Who might know others who could get
involved?
Who might support this activity?
Who might fund it? (also relates to
Future How)
Who might be intersted to give
(resources, materials, money) to the
cause?
Who are good hosts?

Future Where
Where are appropriate places to do this
activity?
Where are inappropriate places but would
be good to try?

Future How (could it be organised?)
How can you involve others in
development of knowledge/activity?
How can people get involved a little
bit, more than once, or regularly?
How might the outcomes and outgoings be
kept open for unexpected development?
How might it get messy?

+++ Discussion (15 mins)

What do people want to learn?
Are there overlaps between group's
different wishes?
Where are the gaps in group's proposals?

Lorenza Perelli

HOW TO UNDERSTAND TOMATOS

Introduction:

I. Italian cousine is NOT based on tomatos. If your idea of lasagne is that pasta floating on a sea of red, think again. No, no, no! (spoiler: lasagne, are made with tomato paste - a little)

II. tomato sauce comes from immigration from the south, historically. Globalization brought people from central n North of Italy, which mostly DON'T use tomatos, also because they don't grow so wonderful there, like in the south (lucky them, sunny areas). Is that why risotto has become popular? ☺ (failed emoticon...) (spoiler: tomato plants should be NOT given a lot - normal quantity of water. Consider them like succulent! Once you cut your tomato almost NO water should be present). (crazy eh..) mantra: tomato are from SOUTH of Italy... dry, sun only

I'll try to write smaller because I have to
/summarize a lot of info now:

90% of tomato use in italian cousine
came s from TOMATO PASTE.

It give "the color" (tecnical term)
to unify flavors in soup, x ex,

switching pen now...
IF YOU REALLY INSIST OF DOING TOMATO SAUCE FOR PASTA,
(the only acceptable use c:) CONSIDER:

i. whole tomato   └ other failed emoticon
ii. crushed
iii. puree
(obviously ready sauce is out of the question a blasphemy, sorry!)

⇒ RATIO to DECIDE ⇒ QUANTITY of WATER
so option ① → AVOID! too watery. In the south of
Italy tomatos are used fa the sauce in the middle of the
summer, at the pick of the season, and cooked with a
technique I don't have space to tell now, but please
believe me, if I say that chicago in february can not
offer the same circumstances: ☞ No watery sauce,
opening the whole can and just pour it in the pan.
(blasphemy! sorry!)

⇒ USE CRUSHED TOMATOS if you really can't stew away
from having spaghetti with tomato sauce.
CAREFUL NOT TO OVERCOOK ii: FINAL RATIO
90% flesh; 10% water- oh, I almost forgot.
NO "SPICE UP", Italians use very few spices and
almost always from fresh plants. Add to sauce
once it's DONE or it will become ACID

so, I'm running out of space.
one final note: italian cousine is very
UNEXPENSIVE (1 pack pasta; 1 can tomato makes f
a family of 4). AND healty Don't be intimidated,
don't listen to false prophet and you should be
ready to go, as fa most things in life. Peace
and love and food! ❤!

Erik Peterson

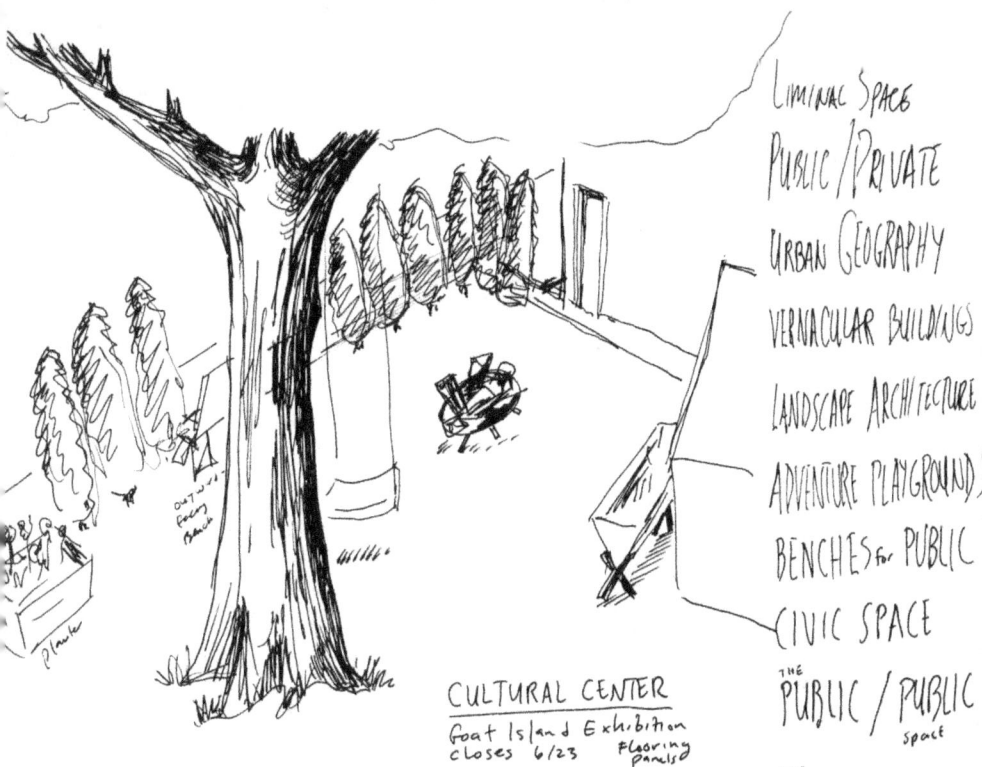

LIMINAL SPACE
PUBLIC / PRIVATE
URBAN GEOGRAPHY
VERNACULAR BUILDINGS
LANDSCAPE ARCHITECTURE
ADVENTURE PLAYGROUNDS
BENCHES for PUBLIC
CIVIC SPACE
THE PUBLIC / PUBLIC space

THE FUNCTION of PLACES
SITE as PLATFORM
ENGAGE while "OFF"
ZONED COMMERCIAL / ZONED RESIDENTIAL
RAIL / STREET
EVENT SCULPTURES
OUTWARD FACING
DIY ILLEGAL CAMP
ARCHITECTURAL / INTERVENTION
PROTOTYPES

PARTNERS

COMPOUND YELLOW (LAURA) SHAEFFER

LATHROP COOPERATIVE WOODSHOP (ERIK + BRYAN) - 2 day / week
Thursdays

AFTERSCHOOL MATTERS (LUKE) JOYNER

CABINETS / KITCHEN (MEJAY) GULA
DESIGN PROCESS

FIELD TRIPS

Dan Sullivan's shop

sweetwater Fdn

Lathrop / meet w/ Sarah? w/ Jaques?

Tender House - Mejay Gula

Amber Ginsberg - Kiln House

CULTURAL CENTER
Goat Island Exhibition
closes 6/23   Flooring
Panels

KIDS / APPRENTICES

20 kids
9th - 12th Grade

TIME

Monday - Thursday
9am - 1pm

DATES

week 1   6/24 - 6/27   (cultural Ctr/ (Lathrop on Thurs))

week 2   7/9 - 7/11

week 3   7/15 - 7/18
week 4   7/22 - 7/25
week 5   7/29 - 8/1
week 6   8/5 - 8/8

155

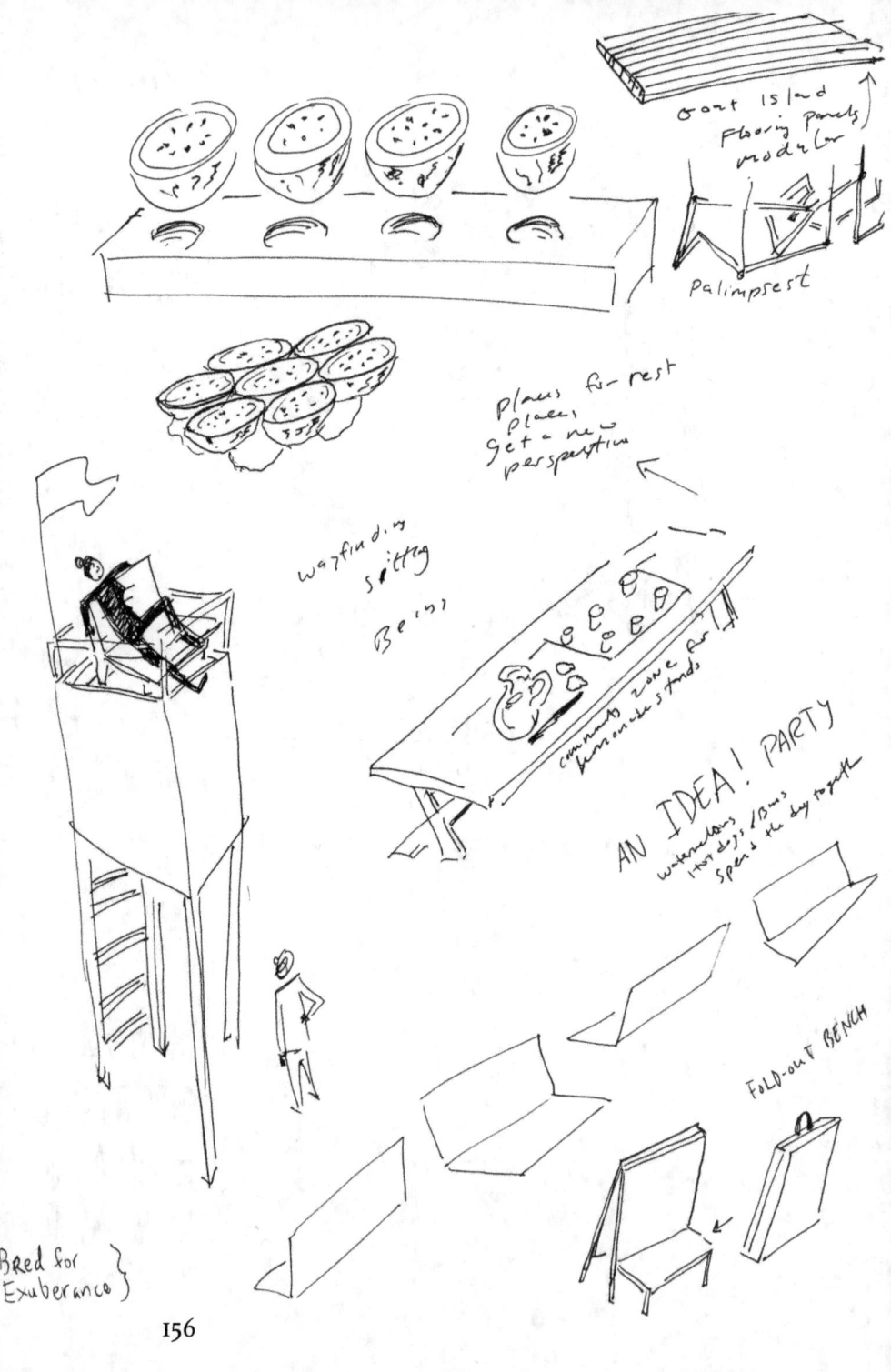

Goat Island
flooring panels)
modular

Palimpsest

places for rest
places
get a new
perspective

wayfinding
sitting
Being

community zone for
homemade stands

AN IDEA! PARTY
watermelons/chs
hotdogs/chs
spend the day together

FOLD-OUT BENCH

Bred for
Exuberance

156

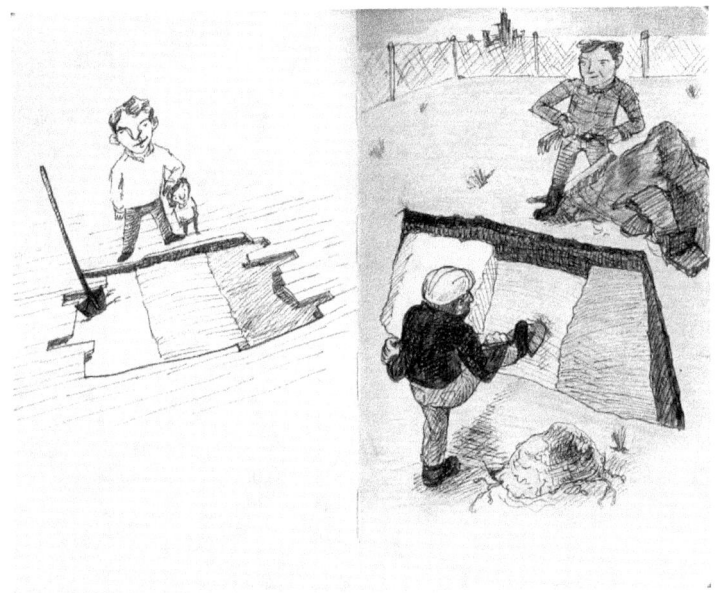

Neapolitan Excavation

Please feel free to color the Neapolitan layers with chocolate, vanilla, and strawberry colored crayons (or get creative and choose your own favorite flavors)!

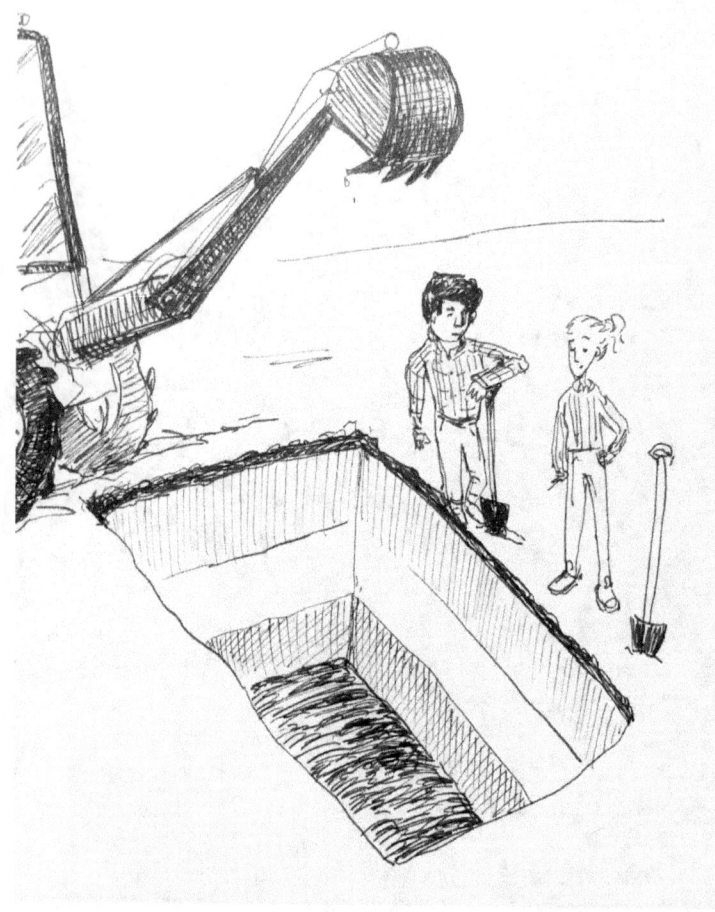

Neapolitan Excavation

Please feel free to color the Neapolitan layers with chocolate, vanilla, and strawberry colored crayons (or get creative and choose your own favorite flavors)!

Melissa Potter

MARY BLOOD'S
KEFIR MADNESS

••

Probiotic elixir for misogny-induced illnesses!

RECIPE

Take kefir grains and put in bottom of glass jar. Pour whole or 2% milk (goat or cow) over grains and cover jar with coffee filter and rubber band. Place in dark cabinet for 24 - 36 hours. When the milk thickens and slightly curdles, it can be strained through a sieve or plastic strainer and put in the refrigerator for up to five days. The amount of milk added depends on the amount of grains: 1 tablespoon is approximately 2 cups worth. Grains can be reused and grow over time!

Things you can grow when you don't have a yard
By Melissa H Potter, papermaker, feminist, collaborator:
Seeds InService

I've never had real yard space. For a hot second, I had a
shoebox size of really battered soil in the front of a Jersey
City house. I have always wanted to grow, so I used that
space with no idea what I was doing. A peony flourished,
despite it all. I had no idea at the time soil is a universe.
Mine had been wrecked by urbanization.

Many years later, I had the incredible opportunity to farm
at The Papermaker's Garden, a 10-bed garden at 8th and
Wabash in Chicago, IL. My school built it on an entire
city lot. And it was more work than students could
manage, so my collaborator, Maggie Puckett and I took
over 5, 4' x 25' beds and Seeds InService was born.

The school tore down that space to make way for a
student center, and I began making jokes about
conceptual gardening. It really wasn't a joke: gardening is
about more than dirt, it's about cultivating the mind,
making connections, and understanding the metaphors of
interconnectedness and interdependency of miraculous
invisible worlds. Over time, however, I realized we can
grow in almost any place and engage with varied
microbiomes.

Many apartments do not have enough light to grow
plants. Seedlings have a hard time flourishing in this
environment. I eventually got a grow light, and set up a

station on my refrigerator. Some live things love darkness and cozy spots out of reach. I will talk about them below!

I believe when we grow live things, we deepen our compassion and our understanding of the world around us.

Some things I've experimented with, under the title, *Fermentation for Feminism!*:

Kombucha
My interest in kombucha was born from two bodies of research: a papermaking experiment with an IIT graduate student, Alex Eisenberg, turning SCOBY into micro-cellulose and a theoretical experiment inspired by anthropologist, Larisa Jasarevic. Kombucha, a fizzy drink made from SCOBY Mother (Symbiotic Culture of Bacteria and Yeast) has been used as a magical health elixir and became incredibly popular in countries like Bosnia where there was little access to medicine during war. In 2017 – 18, We had huge vats of it growing in the Columbia College Chicago papermaking studio, and it inspired graduate thesis work, as well as an art installation by the Nietas de Nonó for a major exhibition.

Scoby Syllabus / How to Make The Mother*
Boil 8 - 10 black tea bags / gallon of water. Cool and add 1 cup sugar. Pour into inoculated glass jar leaving 1" approximately at the top. With very clean hands place The Mother at the top. Cover with coffee filter. Put in warm part of the kitchen. Ferment 7 days. Can perform second ferment, or drink.

Share The Mother.

*The mother is a common name for the skin-like, leathery SCOBY that ferments the water, as it is generative.

Reading
Jasarevic, Larisa. 2015. The thing in a jar: mushrooms and ontological speculations in post-Yugoslavia. Cultural Anthropology. 30 (1): 36-64.

Kefir
Kefir is so easy to grow, but you will need to get grains. Grains multiply as they ferment milk, and you can share them! You can also try to source them from another person making kefir. (We are a subculture around you.) Milk kefir is much easier to grow than water kefir. I experimented quite a bit with water kefir, but found the Chicago water very challenging due to heavy mineralization.

After much study on Mary Blood, founder of Columbia College Chicago, I created a fictional series of home remedies in her honor. One of them is attached here with her image. Mary Blood co-founded Columbia College Chicago as a school of oratory for women to amplify their voices before the dawn of women's liberation in the late 1800s.

John Preus

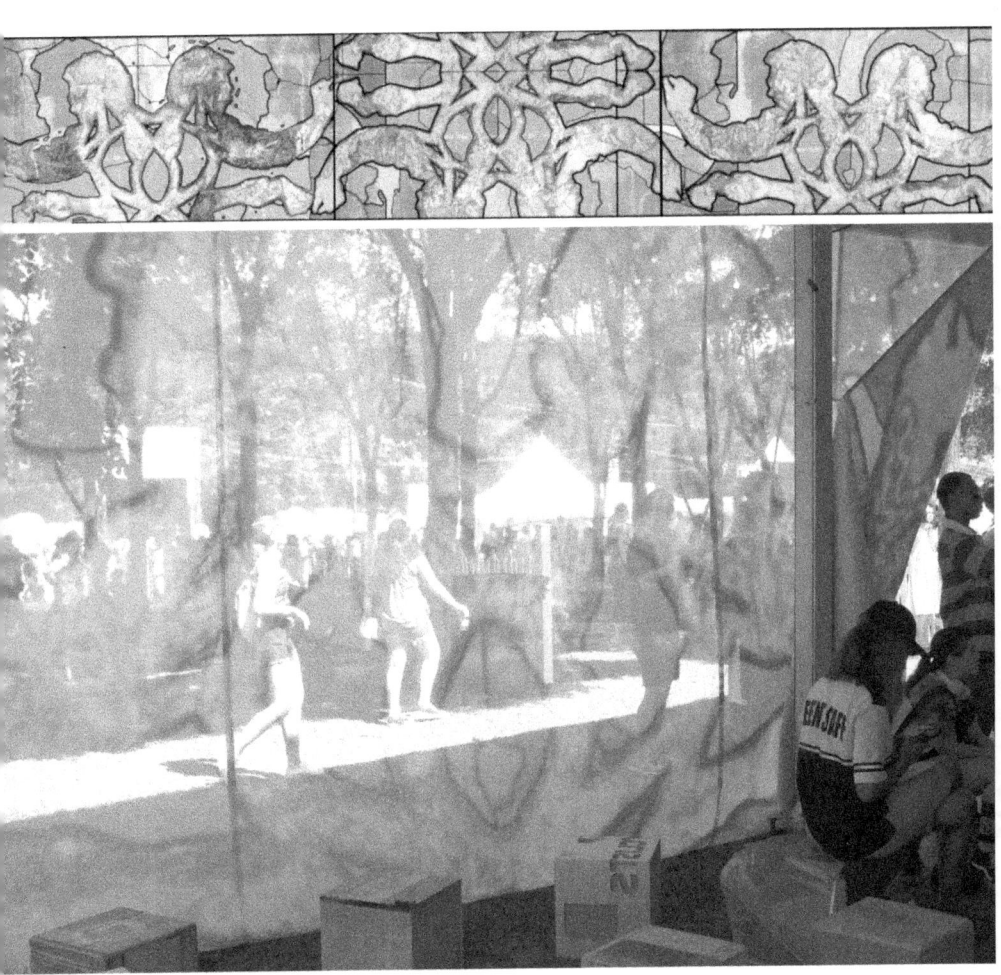

Holding Pattern
Plan for clerestory windows in a municipal building
scale variable.

Pictured here on mesh screen for cultural center
performance tent – Taste of Chicago, 2019

Public Collectors

A Recipe for a Meal-Based Artist Residency Program

We can create informal structures that will enable the positive experiences we want to have in our cities. They don't have to cost a lot of money and the scale can be whatever we want it to be. To this end, in August 2016, I launched a meal-based artist residency program under the authorship and administration of my project Public Collectors. I wanted to make myself available as a resource to other artists, share something great in my neighborhood and enjoy meaningful conversations over food, outside of an institutional or academic context.

The Public Collectors Joong Boo Residency Program consisted of me buying Korean lunch for the resident and sharing a meal with them at Joong Boo Market on 3333 N. Kimball Avenue in Chicago. A residency typically lasted an hour but some were much longer. I hosted 38 residents in just under two years. There were artists I knew but hadn't seen in a decade, artists I barely knew or had never met, or artists I've seen many times but have never spoken with more than fifteen minutes or so at an exhibition opening or event. That residency project is detailed in the publication

The Meal-Based Artist Residency Program, published by Public Collectors in August 2018.

The following text from that booklet provides a list of factors to consider when starting a meal-based residency. It is intended for others who want to apply this model for their own projects.

Factors to Consider When Starting a Meal-Based Artist Residency:

Why: Why do you want to do this? What experience do you want to give people? What are your expectations for the project?

Application: What is the application process? Who do you hope will apply? What do you want to know about potential residents and what do you want to tell them before they apply? How will you circulate the application or information about the project? How might the ways the application circulates influence who your applicants will be?

Location: Where does the residency happen? Is the site easy for you to get to? Is the site easy to get to for a resident that might be taking public transportation? Are there other interesting things in close proximity to the residency site that might be appealing to visit with the resident, or for the resident to see on their own?

Ease of Scheduling: Is the site open every day of the week? Are reservations required? Is there often a long wait?

Dietary Restrictions: Does the residency site offer selections for people on special diets? Are there vegetarian, vegan, and gluten-free options?

Cost: Can you afford to pay for your residency program? Is the food expensive? Does the restaurant serve alcohol? Do you want to make alcohol a feature of your residency? How many people do you want to feed per meal?

Economic Support: Over time, you will spend a considerable amount of money at the residency site. What kind of business do you want to support? Who should benefit from your residency budget?

Frequency: How often do you want to offer residencies? How often can you be available?

Duration: How long should the residency last? How much time do you want to spend with the resident? Are there other things you might do together before or after the meal? Is the site an appropriate location for the amount of time you want to spend?

Outcome: Does the residency have a specific outcome? What form does it take? What might the resident gain from their experience? What will you take away from hosting the residency?

Future: How long do you want to run a residency program? What kind of relationship will you maintain with the residents after their residency? Can past residents reapply? If yes, after how long?

Since the conclusion of the Joong Boo Residency, I have started a new meal-based artist residency: The Courtroom Artist Residency Program. For this I bring artists to observe Criminal Court proceedings in Chicago (usually for several hours) and then we discuss what we observed nearby over lunch at Taqueria El Milagro in Chicago's Little Village neighborhood. In total, I spend at least six hours with each artist between court, the meal, and transit. The conversations have been deeper, and—unsurprisingly—the experiences have been more intense. Our observations have included everything from hearings for a victim of police torture to the murder trial of ex-Chicago police officer Jason Van Dyke, to common daily check-ins and hearings for numerous defendants with drug cases. The residency conversations are recorded, transcribed, and edited for a series of booklets titled The Courtroom Artist Residency Report, published by Public Collectors and available from www.halfletterpress.com. To date there have been sixteen residents and four booklets. You can learn more about this work or contact me with questions at: www.publiccollectors.org. If you start your own residency program, I would love to hear about it.

— Marc Fischer / Public Collectors
March 2020

Maggie Queeney

The Self-Portrait Poem

You will need something to write on, something to write with, and a timer.

The Personality Test

Answer each of the following questions about yourself. For each question, set a timer for 1.5 minutes and write your response, in prose, without stopping. Try to write for the entire time. Don't worry about word choice or if you start to wander from the original topic. The goal is to get ideas onto the page.

1. Who are you?
2. If you could be any animal, what animal would you be?
3. If you could be any color, what color would you be?
4. If you could be any sound, what sound would you be?
5. What texture are you?
6. What movement is most like you?
7. If you could be any space (cupboard, canyon, church, etc.) what space would you be?
8. What object are you?

9. What do you want to be?
10. What are you not?

Set your writing aside for a bit.

Read a few of the following self-portrait poems out loud. If there are people with you, take turns reading a poem out loud. After each a poem is read out loud, close your eyes and then take a minute to write down the words you remember from the poem.

<u>Poems to Read:</u>
- "Self Portrait," Cynthia Cruz
- "Self-Portrait at Ten," Roxane Beth Johnson
- "Self-Portrait as So Much Potential," Chen Chen
- "Self-portrait in a Gold Kimono," Henri Cole
- "Self-Portrait as Exit Wounds," Ocean Vuong
- "Self-Portrait as Artemis," Tarfia Faizullah

After reading and discussing at least three poems, look over the list of words you remembered. What kind of words did you remember? How would you describe them? What do they have in common? Why do you think you remembered these words?

Go through your answers to the personality test. What words are similar to the words you remembered in other poems? Circle them.

Write a poetry self-portrait using the words that you have circled, that starts with the response you wrote that most surprised you. Your poem should present a true portrait, and not contain any biographical information.

Allison Peters Quinn

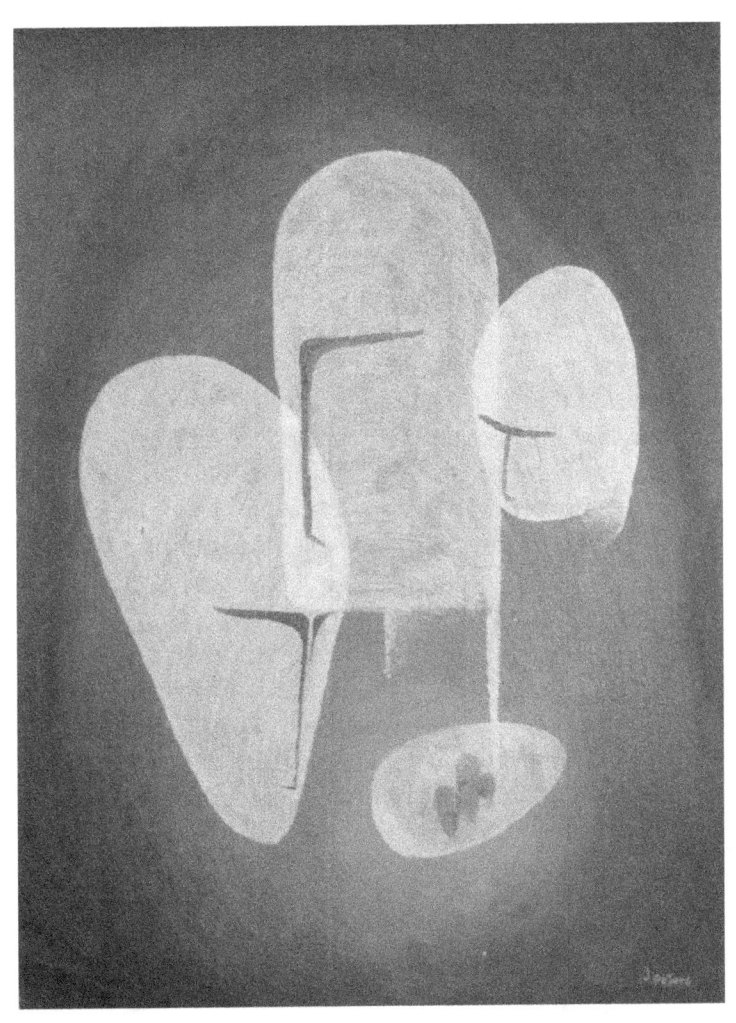

Active Looking

Learning engages the ability to question given facts, dwell in the discomfort of not knowing and form a new understanding of the world around us. The act of concentrated looking, especially repeated and over time, is a simple act of learning.

Inspired by Compound Yellow's aptness for generating lists and wordplay, this contibution offers the image prior as a prompt for free association. The image is of a painting by my father that hung in my childhood home. By seeing it over and over, through decades, the painting taught me that a rewarding visual experience has no answers. The experience of looking opens up a portal of interrogation into the emotional, psychological, and cultural references that surface in the process.

What was the first artwork, film, song, that caused you to experience it repeatedly and each time offered a new level of understanding? Go back, experience it again.

Id
Ego
Super ego
Hypnotism
Alienation
Alien nation
Silent
Interiority
Interdependence

Surveillance
Automaton
Guardians
Big Brother
Family unit
The incredible edible egg
Amniotic
Birth
Conception
Fathomless
Floating
Ghostly
Death
Judgement
Trinity
Origin story
Reincarnation
Regeneration
Lifecycle
Time travel
Futurism
Infinite regress

Alisa Reith & Matthew
Nicholas

***All We Are Is Heat: for the memory of our dearest Bill
Talsma,*** by Alisa Reith and Matthew Nicholas, title
credit to Michael Thomas

I can see your scars
I have them too
The places where they cut
To make us think there was a you, a me, a simple
pronoun
I don't know if you can see it. What I'm seeing
You're sitting too far away and there are too many
others between us for me to approach
And that's the thing
That's it. A big part of it
The excuse
I can't
has been my most successful campaign slogan for
decades
I can't
is labor which I provide to keep my mouth shut
even when I am woke
I can't
should be my legal name
I can't
should be the digits you dial when you wanna call
me text me
to make sure that I am still can't-ing
What a fog

A fog so thick I am amazed I can even see these
things on you on me
that I can even remember
that I am just a pronoun
I am they
is us and thus
I am in a moment of trust
I am walking
I feel like I am seeing but am I
I toil with doubt to make it for better or for worse
Doubt becomes a vehicle that I am tethered to
A vehicle that I am forced into by the me that I
that is the
I can't let myself be myself
because my self was designed ahead of me and that
it is not me
So this is fraught with a doubt of what is better of
what is worse of a feeling a worry
Will I ever be hungry enough to not can't anymore?
To know that I might be too afraid to tell you that I
want to be real but I can't

Pause

Here now

Pause

Let's shift

Pause

This will now be a gesture to our love and being

Of energy consumed of energy expelled and
consumed and expelled
When there are no words left
A flickering of hope
A wavering of desire
Until exhausted and then we must
Only listen

David Schalliol

Find something new in a place you know well: maybe it's around the corner, maybe it's 1,000 miles away, maybe it's under the refrigerator, maybe it's in your heart.

Katrin Schnabl

Instruction for a custom-form pattern-shaping improvisation.

You need:

- An object.

(Alternatively, this can be used to study a custom fit for a bust, hip yoke, or body part*)

- A piece of light-weight cloth large enough to cover the object fully.

(If a muses' bust, or hip, a t-shirt can be used.)

- Generous amounts of masking tape in 1" and 1.5".

- Black and colored permanent marker, pencils and eraser.

And later:
- paper to transfer patterns to;
- fabric or cloth, repurposed or dead-stock, vinyl, tarp, or similar
- sewing supplies/ equipment
- optional closures, such as zipper.

Steps:

1. Cover the object/ body area with suitable cloth.

2. Decide on a central horizon line/ circumference all around the object/ subject and indicate with marker. Tape masking tape over horizon line**; remark on masking tape. Line should be a plain orbit without any points or waves.

3. Cover the entire object by catching at least 1/8"-1/4" of the previous tape; work your way parallel upwards, and then downwards completely covering the object. You may have to cinch the tape as the object tapers or changes shape. Keep taping, snug, but not tight. In the process you create a second skin over the object.

4. Decide on placement for a line perpendicular** to the first line and indicate with marker over masking tape shell. Again, line should make a plain orbit without coming into any point or waves. You should be able to see the two lines you marked intersecting at a right angle in two places on your fully cover piece.

5. Now cover the entire piece with tape in cross-wise direction to first full taping, parallel on both sides of the perpendicular line.

6. Tape a third layer of masking tape over the entire form, going in one direction from one end to the other end. Smooth down the

previous two layers, flatten out any bubbles, and ensure that you get all the shaping around your object.

7. Decide where the cover ideally should open/ close over the object. The length of this line needs to be more than half of the widest circumference to be able to take this cover off, as well as to place any cover you make over the object again. Draw this line on the third masking tape line, and label it opening. You will eventually carefully cut along this line.

8. Before you take the piece off mark any peculiarities: any points, also concavities, curves, etc. that you need later to identify placement. Use the pencil first, and different color permanent markers later, once you are sure about the indicators you want to include.

9. IMPORTANT CARE: Be careful when cutting, slide a clear ruler under the scissor to not damage or hurt the object/ subject underneath

Take the cover off. This is your template. By adhering to a few more steps you can remake his shape from a variety of materials.

You can cut and re-assemble this cover any way you like. It will make the same shape, though you can experiment with different lines. Follow a few important steps:

Any area you can lay flat can be a pattern piece to be cut from fabric. You should cut your dimensional shape in such a way that all the taped pieces can lay flat. Essentially you are transferring the information to recreate the shell of your shape to a flat piece of paper. This would be your block, or your draft at this stage.

10. Trace each piece onto paper. Label each piece. Leave space around it for both notes, and for seam allowance. (Once you have traced all pieces you could also carefully tape it back together, and mark up different cut lines for another variation. Place it back over original volume, and secure with masking tape.)

11. For the pattern you need to:
    a. mark which pieces go together, and where; using notches
    b. labels the seams in a progression you can follow, and mark any and all points such as 1,2,3 and A,B,C
    c. create a diagram that you can follow along
    d. add the same amount of seam allowance (if in fabric) to both pattern pieces sides that come together as a seam

e. before you cut in your material, 'walk' each seam to check that your indicators (notches) are in the right place, and that the markings are correct and go together

*this may take significant time, especially the first time! Practice repeatedly to understand how this could be applied to more refined fittings such as on a human body.

**the horizontal and vertical line gives spatial orientation to your piece that will become critical when you try to reorient individual cut-up pieces. These lines allow you an upper/ lower distinction, as well as left/ right. I find these two absolutely necessary to avoid lengthy backtracking. Feel free to add a third perpendicular line, which intersects at the 'bellies' of the other two circumferences for the sagittal plane (adding a front/ back).

Test your shape, and adjust, as needed.

Then you're ready to explore the shape in various explorations and improvisations including materials, style-lines for the seams, surface, and in-seam options. Have fun.

Doug Shaeffer

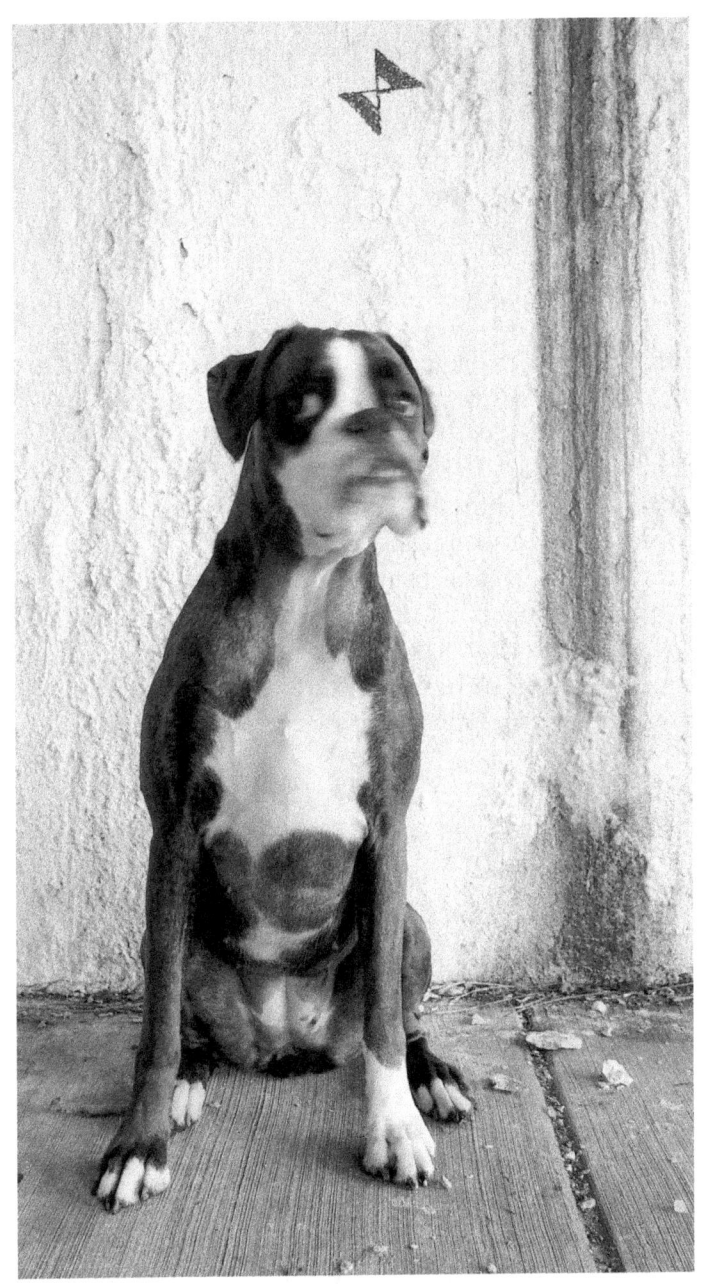

think abject think fear think like zombie story think
like virus like dorcas says think spirit-stunned think
dead think walk think stuck in time think biding
time think capture think in dog time think in entry
think in exit think in amber time think in drain
time think in seep think leech think erode think
flush think breath think futile think i can't think
think the final coup think the final trump think the
opposite of what is is what i think will it be caught
in sci-fi think web think simper fie think endless
think end think money think time think finity.

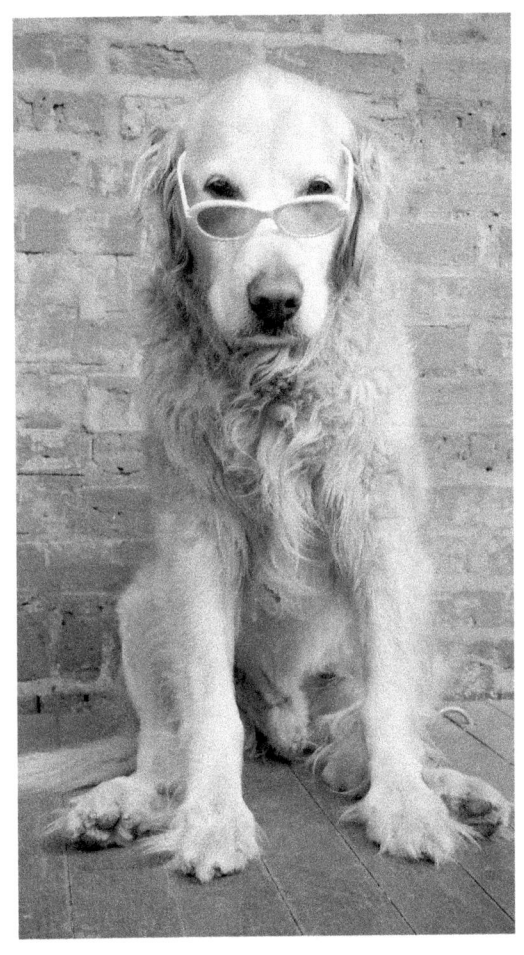

Laura Shaeffer

For the past four years I have worked as a caregiver to a 91 year old man, Charles F. Custer, who became an unexpectedly dear friend. In an attempt to merge my work as a caregiver in a senior center with my life as an artist, I began a daily drawing practice focusing on the human beings, including Charles, with whom I had most contact. Here are a few examples which represent different parameters I had set for myself in this process of observing; examples taken from a daily practice of drawing as a means of being with.

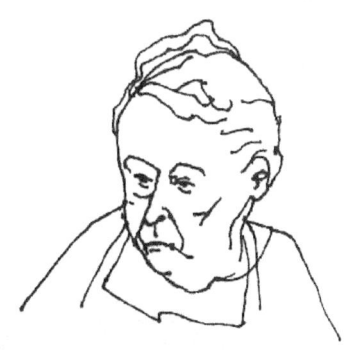

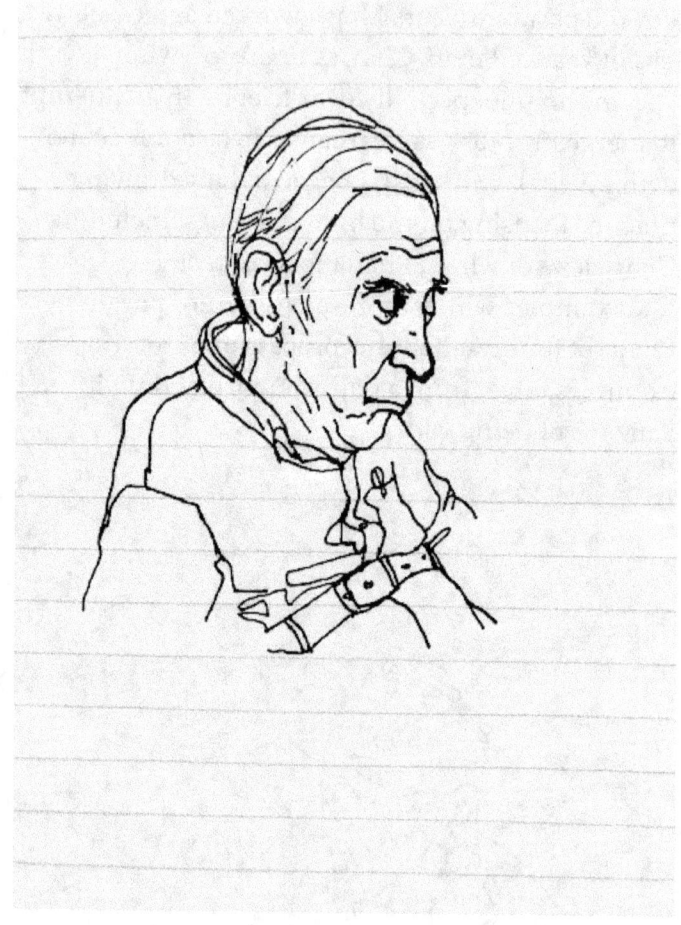

FREE RADICALS

By Alice Munro

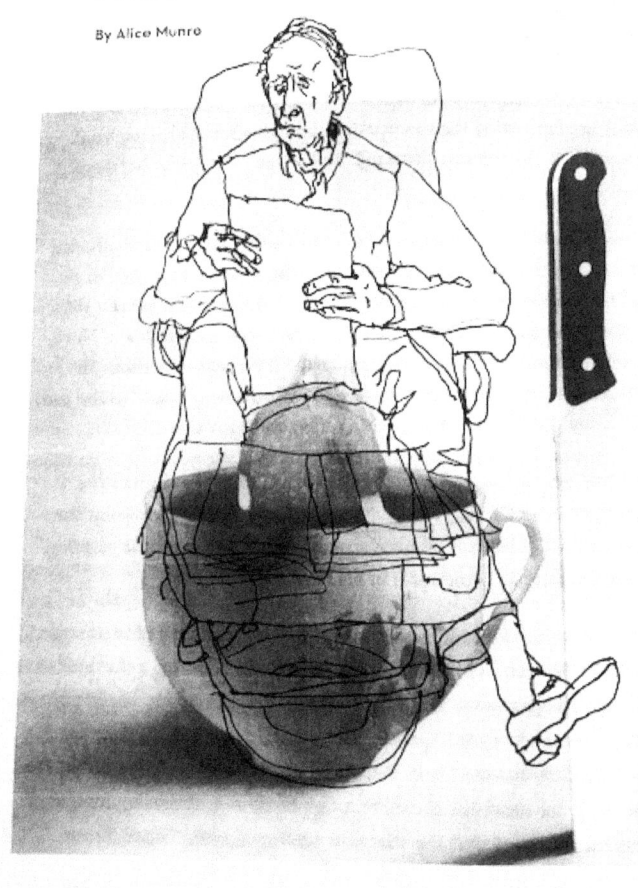

1) Draw with your non-dominant hand.

2) Draw someone sleeping, secretly, with your non-dominant hand.

3) Draw someone secretly, with your non-dominant hand, on random found paper.

4) Draw people secretly, with your non-dominant hand, trying not to pick your pen up from the paper.

5) Draw someone secretly, with your non-dominant hand, with a felt tip pen, trying not to pick your pen up from the paper, use the underdrawing as the drawing.

6) Draw from memory.

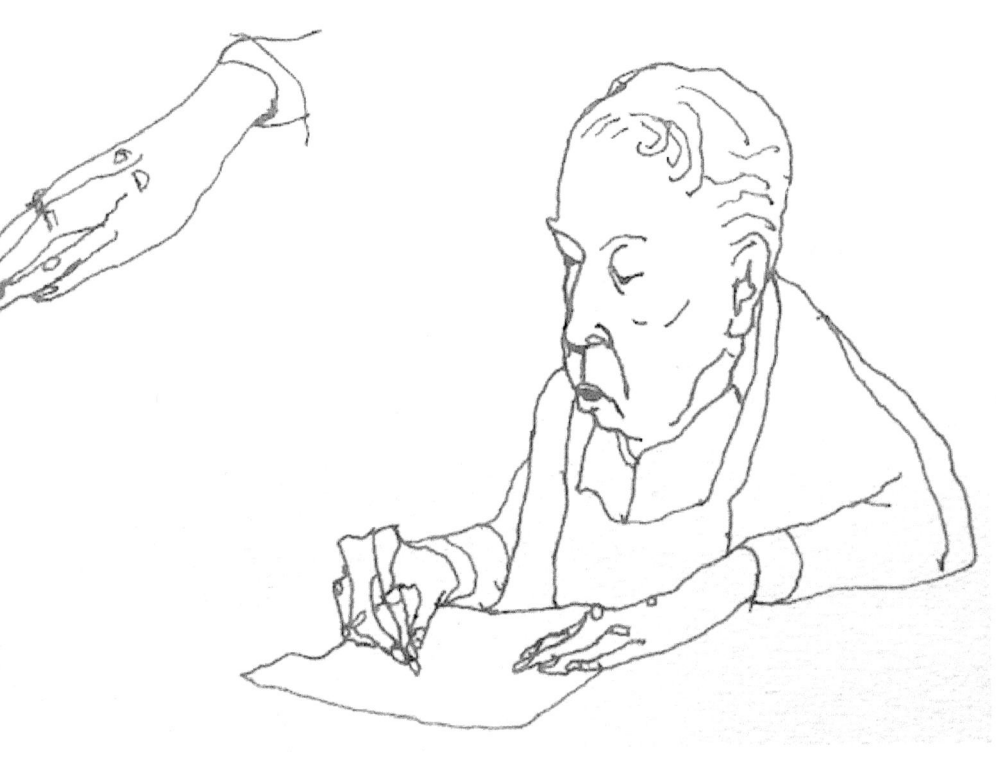

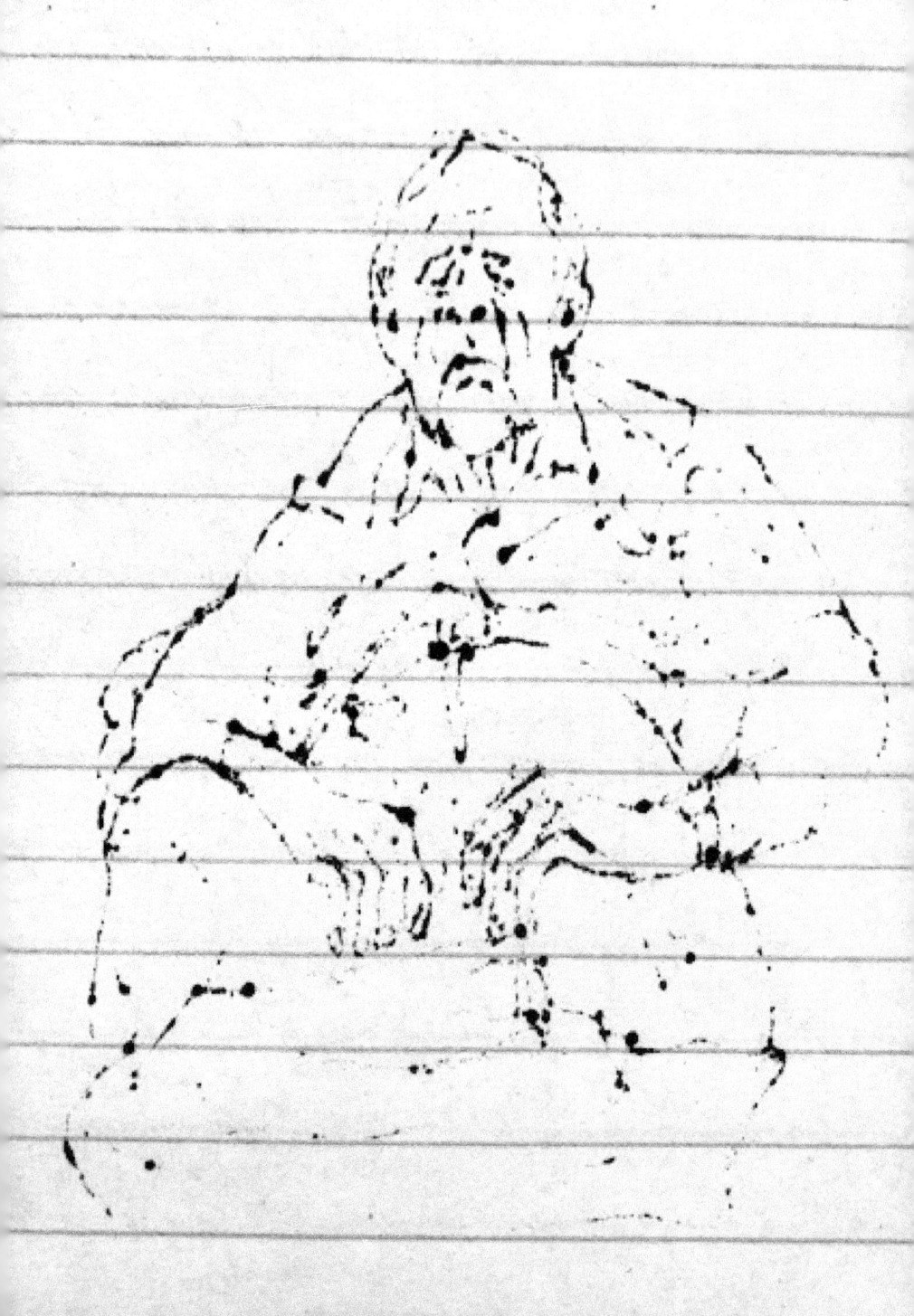

ONE GIGGLE AFTER ANOTHER

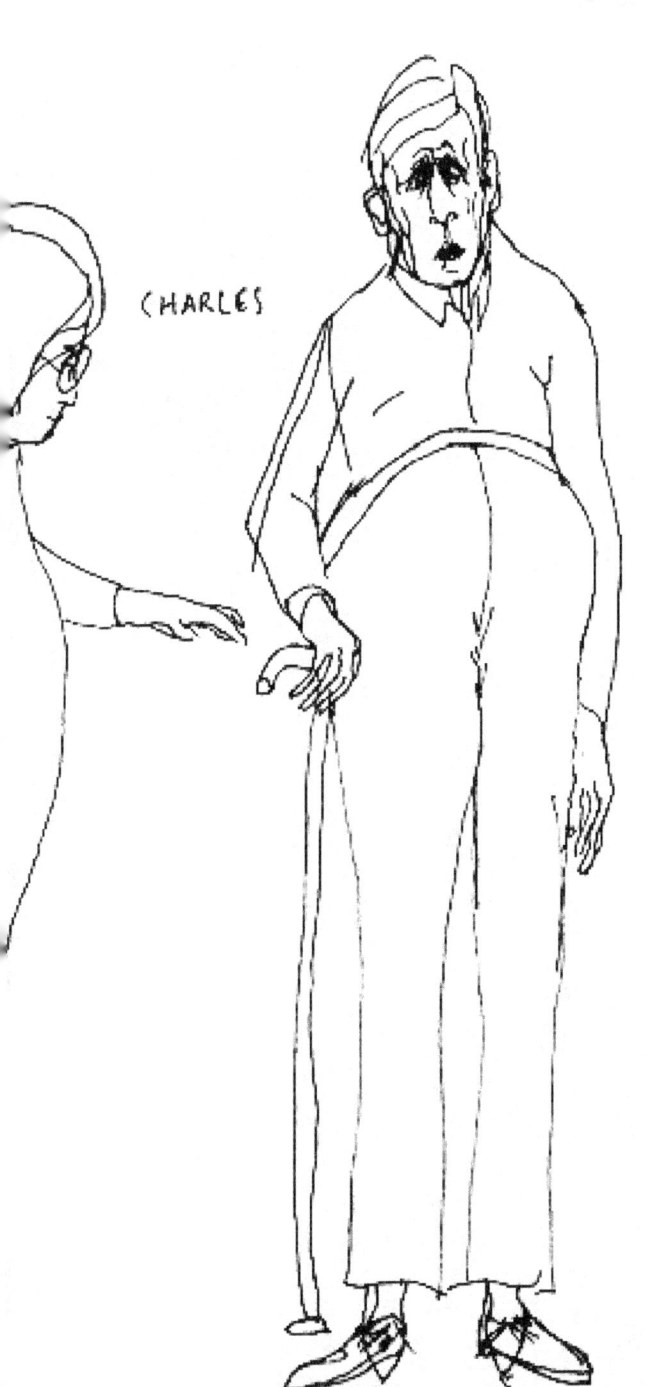

CHARLES

Edra Soto

PINEAPPLE UPSIDE-DOWN CAKE

INGREDIENTS

1 YELLOW CAKE MIX

1 1/4 CUP PINEAPPLE JUICE FROM PINEAPPLE'S CAN

1/2 CUP BUTTER AT ROOM TEMPERATURE FOR CAKE MIX

3 EGGS FOR CAKE MIX

1/2 CUP BUTTER FOR TOPPING

1/2 CUP PACKED BROWN SUGAR FOR TOPPING

9 - 15 SLICES PINEAPPLE FROM TWO 14-OZ. CAN

9 - 15 MARASCHINO CHERRIES WITHOUT STEMS

1 TEASPOON CINNAMON

1/2 TEASPOON VANILLA

DIRECTIONS

PREHEAT OVEN TO 350 DEGREES. BUTTER BOTTOM AND SIDES OF 9" SQUARE BAKING PAN. SPRINKLE WITH BROWN SUGAR. ARRANGE PINEAPPLE RINGS OVER BROWN SUGAR. PLACE CHERRY IN CENTER OF EACH PINEAPPLE RING.

PREPARE CAKE MIX WITH PINEAPPLE JUICE, 1/2 CUP ROOM TEMPERATURE BUTTER AND EGGS ACCORDING TO PACKAGE DIRECTIONS. DIVIDE IN HALF. POUR HALF (ABOUT 2 CUPS) OVER PINEAPPLE AND CHERRIES. USE OTHER HALF AS DESIRED (BAKE SEPARATELY OR USE IN SECOND UPSIDE-DOWN CAKE RECIPE).

BAKE CAKE AT 350 DEGREES FOR 45-50 MINUTES, UNTIL TOOTHPICK INSERTED IN CENTER COMES OUT CLEAN. IMMEDIATELY PLACE HEATPROOF SERVING PLATE UPSIDE DOWN OVER PAN; TURN PLATE AND PAN OVER. LEAVE PAN OVER CAKE A FEW MINUTES SO BROWN SUGAR MIXTURE DRIZZLES OVER CAKE; REMOVE PAN. SERVE WARM (OR COLD). STORE CAKE LOOSELY COVERED.

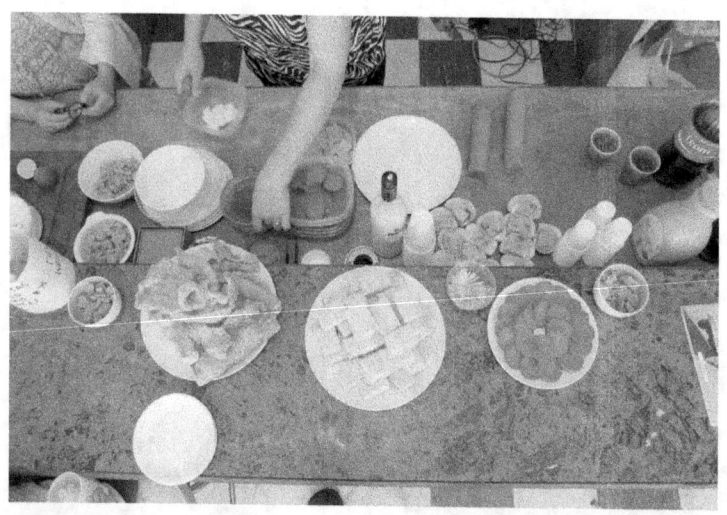

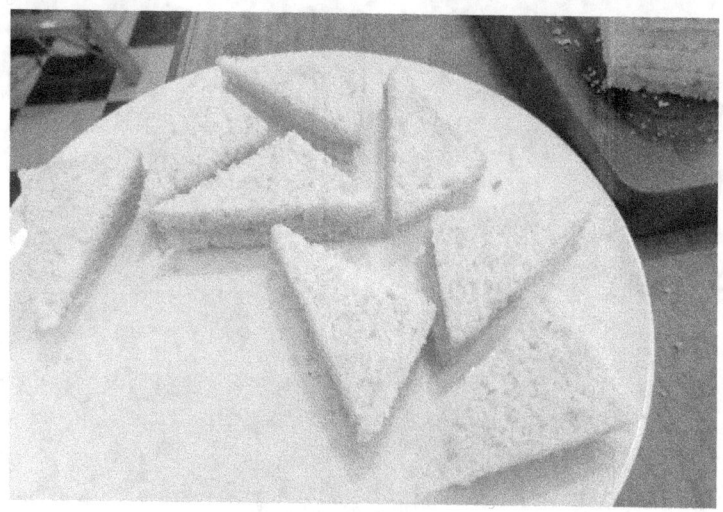

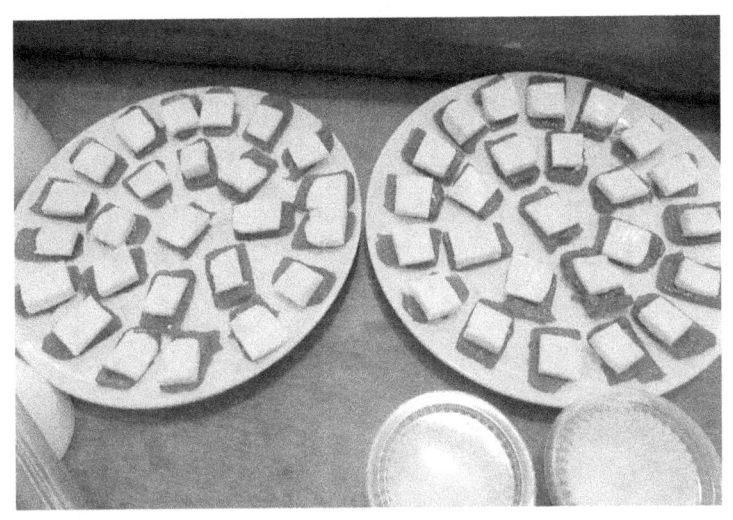

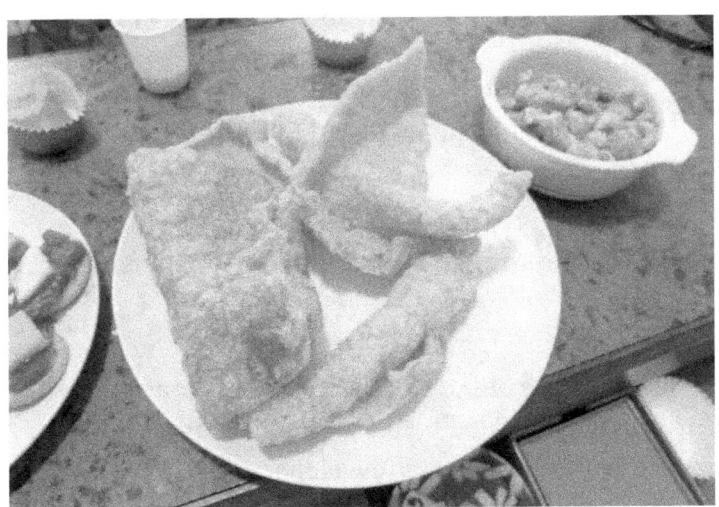

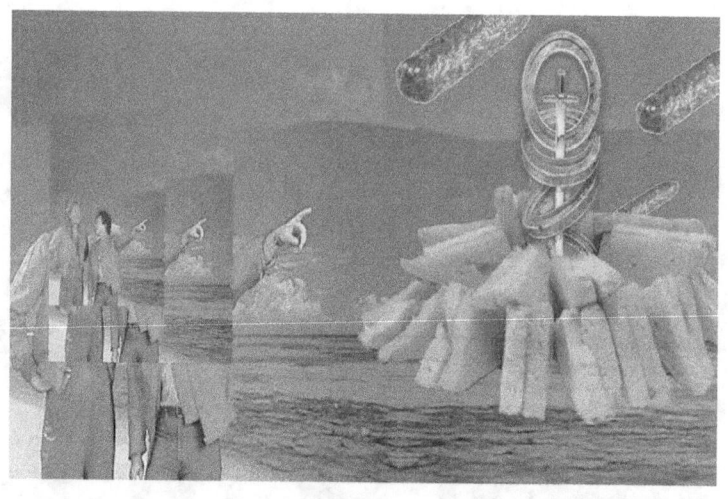

Puerto Rican artist Edra Soto welcomes you to
Happy Hour, a program of hors'd oeuvres she
enjoyed at social gatherings while growing up in
Puerto Rico during the 80's era.

This food is considered the hybridized Puerto
Rican diet strongly influenced by mainstream
American culture.
Romanticized processed foods that became the
centerpiece of Puerto Ricans entertainment.
A fantasy created by marketing becomes tradition.
Adventurous eaters are welcomed!

Puerto Rican born, Edra Soto is an interdisciplinary
artist, and co-director of the outdoor project space
THE FRANKLIN. Recent exhibits include Museum

of Contemporary Art of Chicago; Perez Art Museum, Miami; Museo de Arte de Puerto Rico and Albright Knox Northland, Buffalo. Residencies include Skowhegan School of Painting and Sculpture; Beta-Local; Robert Rauschenberg Foundation; Headlands Center for the Arts; Project Row Houses; and Art Omi. Recent awards include Efroymson Contemporary Arts Fellowship; Illinois Arts Council Grant; 3Arts Residency Fellowship in partnership with Montalvo Arts Center; and the inaugural Foundwork Artist Prize. Her latest commissioned public work titled Screenhouse will be on view at Millennium Park's Boeing Gallery North from 2019 to 2021. Her artwork was included in three exhibitions supported by the MacArthur Foundation's International Connections Fund. Venues include Museo de Arte de Puerto Rico, the Smart Museum; and "Close to There < > Perto de La" to take place in Salvador, Brazil in 2020. Also in 2020 her work will be presented at "Open House: Domestic Thresholds", the inaugural exhibition for the Albright-Knox Northland and at "State of the Art 2020" at Crystal Bridges Museum of American Art. Soto holds a BFA degree from Escuela de Artes Plastics de Puerto Rico. She is a lecturer for the Contemporary Practices Department at the School of the Art Institute of Chicago, from which she received an MFA. www.edrasoto.com

Connie Spreen

Communications technology has proved a useful and potentially life-enhancing tool. Yet, if not attributed its proper value and used under appropriate conditions, this technology induces anxiety in the user, fosters meaningless communication, undermines the quality of human interactions, and renders some of us unable to locate the silence and solitude essential to thinking and to spiritual well-being.

Recognizing these risks, Connie Spreen has established necessary limits on her use of technology. Please be advised that she finds it impossible to:

* Respond to every email message she receives;

* Respond to email messages within the same day;

* Respond to any email messages on Saturday or Sunday;

* Answer the phone only because it is ringing;

* Answer the phone while she is already engaged in conversation with another human being;

* Promise a response to every phone call received.

These limits are intended not to frustrate communication but to deepen it.

Albert Stabler

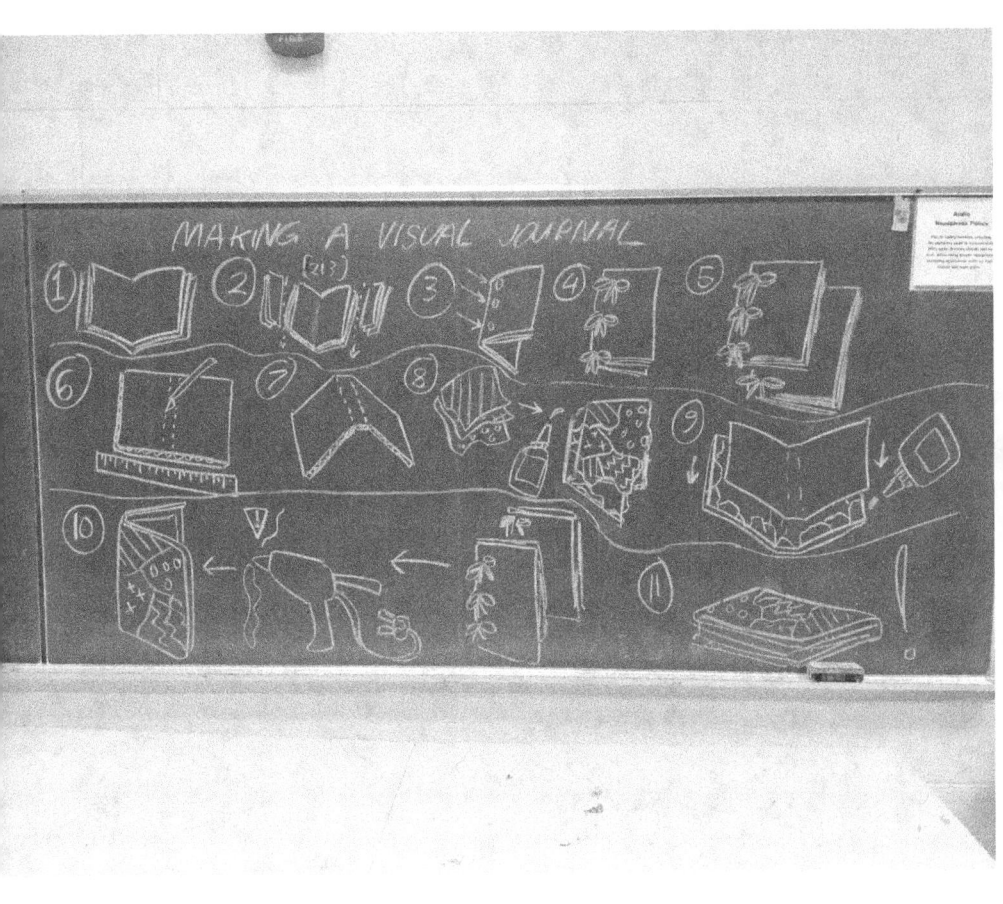

213

CREEL
THE ECO-WALL OF HOPE

ENDANGERED PEOPLE & ANIMALS
MULTI-AGE INTERACTIONS
COMMUNITY TROUBLESHOOTING
DRAWING, CERAMICS, WRITING
PLANNING & DOCUMENTING

air

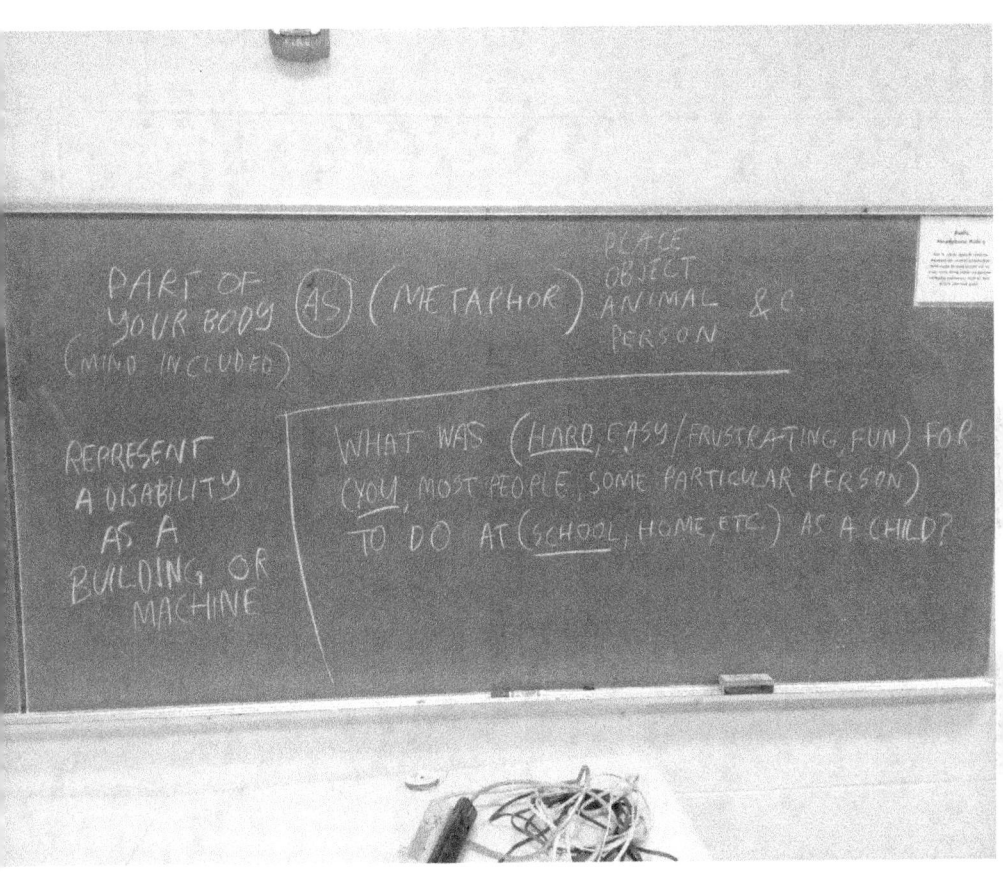

PART OF
YOUR BODY (AS) (METAPHOR) PLACE
OBJECT
ANIMAL &c.
PERSON
(MIND INCLUDED)

REPRESENT
A DISABILITY
AS A
BUILDING OR
MACHINE

WHAT WAS (HARD, EASY/FRUSTRATING, FUN) FOR
(YOU, MOST PEOPLE, SOME PARTICULAR PERSON)
TO DO AT (SCHOOL, HOME, ETC.) AS A CHILD?

MODERN CHILDHOOD IN THE WEST   COLONIZED CHILD.

BIRTH CONTROL ↑, BIRTH RATE ↓, DEATH RATE ↓ PUNISHMENT/ABUSE↓ ──→ NO

→ GENDER DIFFERENTIATION IN SCHOOL, WORK ↓ ──→ NO

LITERACY↑ WORK → SCHOOLING ──────────→ NO

↑ ROLE OF THE STATE ↑, RELIGION ↓ ──────→ YES

FREUD   MORAL INFLUENCE OF PARENTS ──────→ NO

DEVELOPMENT   ADOLESCENCE & CHILDHOOD INVENTED ──→ NO

KIDS AND ADULTS, DIFFERENTIATED ──────→ NO

INDUSTRIALIZATION↑, CHILD LABOR ↓ ──────→ NO

CHILDHOOD SIN → CHILDHOOD INNOCENCE, $$ ──────→ NO

PROTECTION + NURTURING ──────→ ?

PARENTAL CONTROL ↓ SENTIMENTALITY↑ ──→ YES

↓ EXTENDED FAMILY CARETAKERS ──────→ NO

MARRIAGE - BASED UNIT ──────→ NO

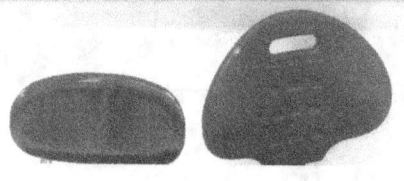

216

(UbD
TEMPLATE
ON
ASULearn)

WHO ARE YOU WITH?

WHAT ARE YOU USING?

WHAT IS THE END RESULT?

WHAT IS THE LARGER POINT? WHY BOTHER?

WHERE ARE YOU?

WHAT WILL HAPPEN, IN WHAT ORDER?

WHAT WILL BE LEARNED OR DISCUSSED?

WHAT STANDARDS ARE ADDRESSED?

HOW WILL YOU KNOW IT WORKED?

DISABILITY
VANDALISM

DiS-HacK

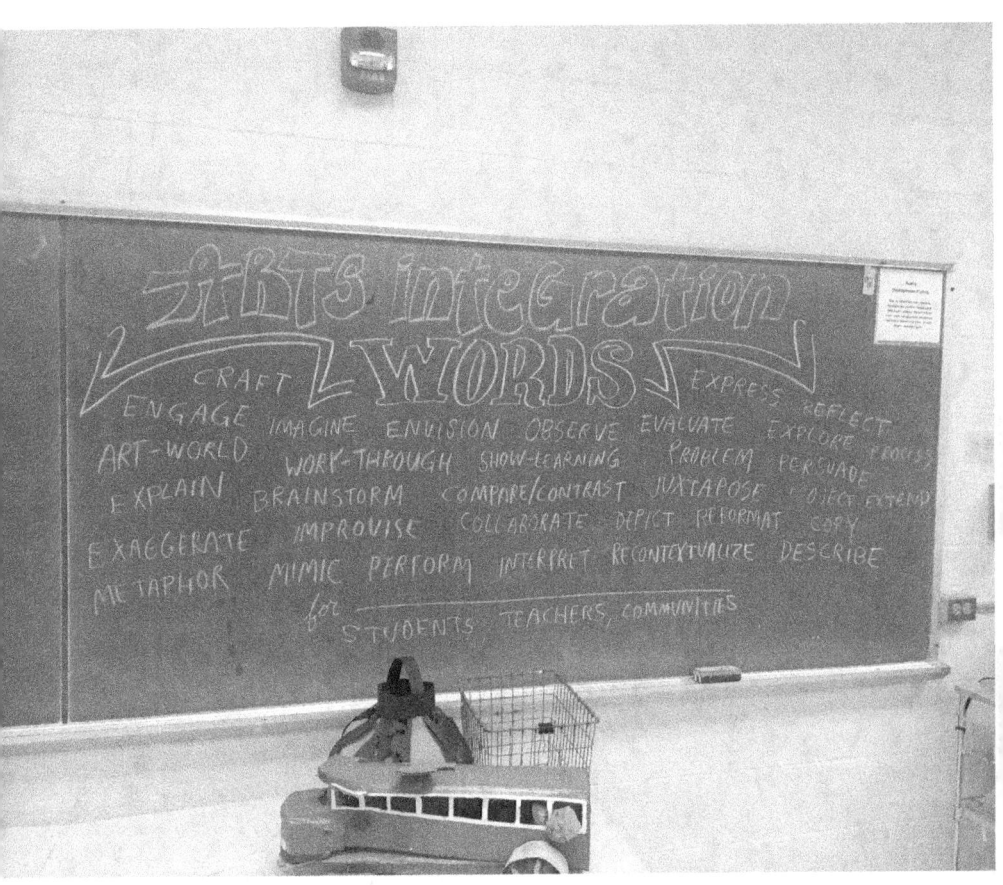

TEACHING CONTEXT

- HOMELIFE
- DISABILITIES
- RACE
- CLASS
- GENDER
- SEXUALITY
- FUNDING
- ADMIN
- PARENTS

- PRECONCEPTIONS OF ART
- CONFIDENCE
- CLASS INCLUSIVITY
  ↳ VIBE
- MATERIALS
  ↳ EQUIPMENT
- MENTAL HEALTH
- SPACE
- CURRICULUM
- ATTENTION SPAN

- AGE GROUP
- EXPERIENCE
- INSTITUTION
- AREA (WIRIS)
- SPACE
- SAFETY
- ENTHUSIASM/INTEREST
- CULTURE
- TEACHER COMMUNITY
- BIASED ART HISTORY

- RE
- SCH
- CURRE
  EVE
- HIS

Randall Szott

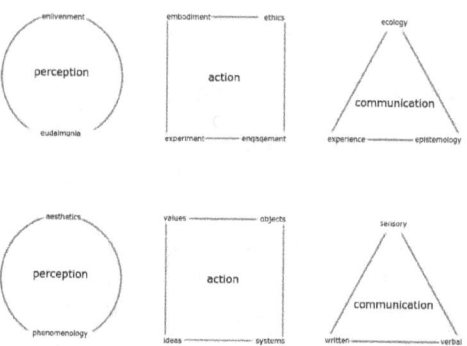

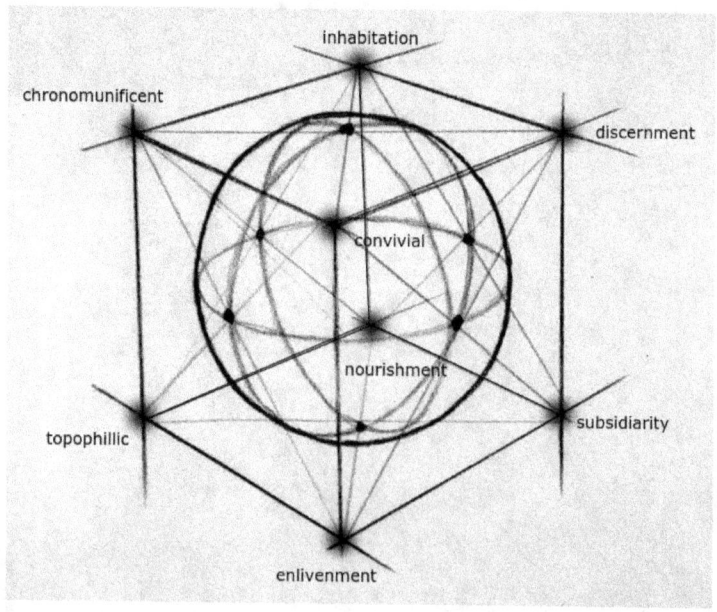

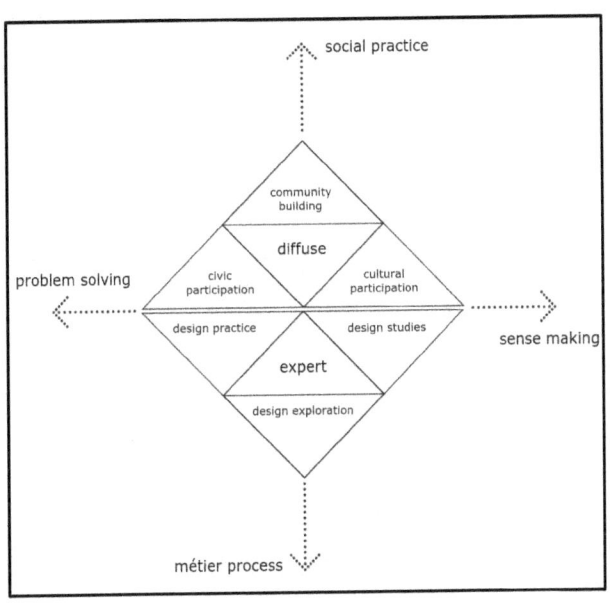

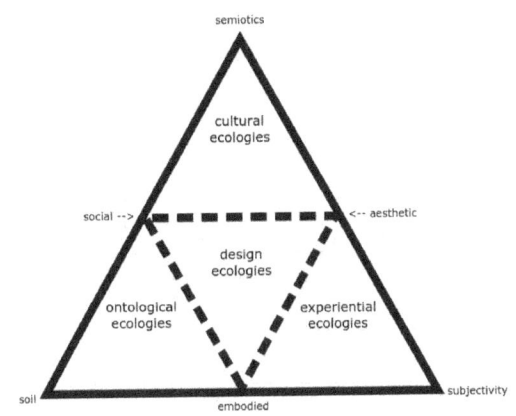

ART SYSTEM (AGRICULTURE)	AESTHETIC ECOLOGY (PERMACULTURE)
Linear	Cyclical
Perpetual "innovation" and growth	Sustainable and regenerative
Boom/bust cycles	Steady state
Concentrated	Distributed
High degrees of specialization	Multiple creative practices
Wealth inequality	Shared resources
Intensive resource use	Low impact
Expert/elite	Amateur/everyday
Value in scarcity	Value in abundance
Antagonism	Interconnection
Brittle infrastructure	Resilient infrastructure
Alters place	Adapts to place
Financial	Ecological
Institutional	Vernacular

Shift in emphasis for #soilpractice + #socialpractice +
#soulpractice education

-->

observation	communion
work	leisure
intellectual	moral
classroom	campfire
knowledge	experience
teaching	learning
cosmopolitan	provincial
specialization	holism
mastery	resilience
abstract	rooted
expertise	wisdom
individuated	social
critique	compassion
analysis	meaning
institutional	improvisational
data	perception
mind	embodiment
colleague	friend
written word	conversation
rational	reasonable
epistemology	aesthetics

Rachel Wallis

How to Make a Map Quilt

Find a map of a place you live or love or that is important to your life. It doesn't have to be a current map, you can find centuries of historical maps of the US on the USGS website (https://www.usgs.gov/core-science-systems/ngp/tnm-delivery/topographic-maps).

Look at the map, think about how the features of it were changed by nature, by climate, by human hands. Think about how they will change in the future. Think about who lived there before you, and where they are now. Think about migrations and watersheds, and industrial footprints. Notice how shape, line, texture, and color interplay on the map.

Print your map out. You can print it at home or much larger at a copy shop, or through a pdf plotting service online. Your map quilt can be the size of a single sheet of paper, or you can tape sheets together indefinitely. Your map quilt will be the size of your paper map.

Transfer the map on to a piece of fabric. You can use a light box to trace the map on a light piece of fabric, or fabric transfer paper (I like Saral). Trace any major lines, like roads, or rivers, or railroads. Trace the edges of the map, to give yourself a frame to work from.

Cut out the prominent shapes from your paper map. They might be mountaintops or lakes, or demographic trends in neighborhoods. Trace these shapes on to fabric – you can try and match the colors of the map but you can also choose a fabric color that looks nice or feels true. Attach the shapes to their correct position on the map. You can sew them on by hand or machine, or use a double-sided fusible web like Wonder Under.

Cut a piece of cotton batting and backing fabric the same size of your fabric map, safety-pin the three layers together, placing pins about a fist-width apart across the map.

Stitch your map, by hand or machine. Use thread or embroidery floss to add texture, to trace waterways and elevation lines, and define neighborhoods or houses. Add beads or tack ribbons or yarn to your map to represent data or the flow of people or water or money. Think about geography as you stitch. Think about the feet that traveled these roads, and why the roads were put where they were. Think of who profited and who was displaced why these structures were created. Think about borders and what they mean. Think about the animals and plants that live along your map. Which ones aren't there anymore? What ones grew up in their place. Ask your friends and neighbors to sew with you, and find out what these landscapes mean to them.

Don't worry that your map is not accurate, that the scale or proportions are off. No one will need to navigate by your map. It doesn't have to be accurate. It just has to be true.

Tessa Windt

CareMake

An invitation to observe your actions and gestures in relation to caring and making over a two-day period.

How you define caring and making will be up to you. You may want to define these terms before you begin and again after you complete the exercise.

On the first day, note down anything you do that you consider to be an act of caring.

On the second day, note down anything you do that you consider to be an act of making.

Compare your two lists; notice any actions or gestures that overlap between caring and making and where you might find opportunities for more overlap to occur. Consider noting existing and new overlaps on a third day.

Send examples to Tessa Windt at twindt@yahoo.com

Sean Ward

Dialogue Exercise: Conjuring meanings

Pick a word for the day. Doesn't need to be complicated. A simple word is fine.

Any word then?

Any word. Sound it out. Let the consonants and vowels roll around in your mouth. Play with the syllables and intonation. Rearrange them. But it's best to keep them in order and manipulate each block's sounds.

Like mispronunciations?

As if you're mispronouncing, but with intention. While playing with your word, write out your revisions like a pronunciation key.

Word = Paper
Pay-purr
Paap-Rr

Think of each pronunciation as a new word and write a definition. Don't limit your new definition based on the original.

Just make up a definition?

Imagine that this new word has an effect on your surroundings, people, things or perhaps it belongs to the supernatural or mythical.

Word = Paper
Pay-purr = a price paid for blankness
Paap-Rr = an owner or guardian of
nostalgia

Use your newly constructed words and definitions today. Log them into a personal dictionary.

Debrief
Dialogue with yourself:
- Using a voice recorder, record yourself saying your new words.
- Make videos of yourself saying your new words. Depending on the definition, it could be you sitting there pronouncing the words or using the word to point out an object with its word.
- Write a few sentences making use of your words as they are defined. Use them in a story, a poem, a letter, or anything you would like to write.
- Define an etymology for each of your words.

Dialogue with others:
Ask a partner to do this exercise and then participate with you in this debrief. Share your words with your partner.
- Using a voice recorder ask your partner to record saying them, you record theirs. Exchange these voice recordings.

- Ask your partner to use your words in a piece of writing. You use theirs to write something. Exchanges these writings. Or record reading the piece of writing and then exchange.
- Ask your partner to create a video using a word or two. It could be in natural conversation with someone, a scripted video, or simply of your partner pronouncing the word. Exchange these videos.

These exchanges can happen in-person or remotely.

Examples

Word = Dream
DUR-eam = an exhausting adventure holding your eyes closed
DAR-Ream = a gathering of people in one's mind
durr-e-mm = a measurement of weight after waking

Word = Robe
Row-Buba = erratic, hasty movements in attempt to cover one's self
Rah-oo-ba = a seduction technique
Row-o-ba = a dance involving loose fitting garments to announce the day

Word = Pillow
Pill-Laow = one of the many creator's names
PILL-ow = a resting point for injuries
Pe-ILL-O = a hollowed call

Word = Rug
RA-ugga = sign of affection towards a
stranger
Rr-u-gah = an object of peace
rrr-aah-UGh = an accelerating tone or
chant done in a gathering of people in
a desperate time of need

Word = Sneaker
Snee-ke-ek-rr = subtle housing
Ss-knee-keek-R = sound of a wet thing
being drained
Sss-knee-Krr = comfortable silence

Word = Tinder
Tin-der = the leftovers or ruins of the
sun

Natalie Wright

rain

on
a
window
lasts
like
this:

!

and keeps moving

!

natalie wright

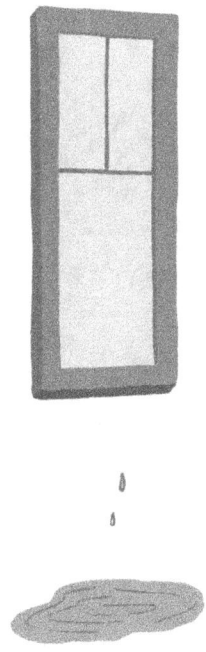

Ji Yang

How to Cook Pigeon

无产者专门教程

VERSION CHICAGO

An Introduction for
Nothing Owners
Contemporary Nomad
Life Stylist
Anti-capitalist
Proletarians

A. The pigeon was first introduced into the country as food and for hunting.

B. A particular kind, rock dove, is very adaptable to the urban environment, so the number starts to grow rapidly, it is a "problem" around the globe.

C. Hunter-gatherer is the true nature of we as the human species. it is proven that a semi-nomadic living style is the best for your soul and the alternative way to cure depression caused by most contemporary issues.

D. Double eco-friendly: economically friendly and ecologically friendly.

E. Free yourself from the deadlock of capitalism.

HUNT.

unting pigeons doesn't require an eagle's strength. it is actually very easy. here is a method suitable for all ages and all body shapes, and the material required can be found in the city.

Step #1: find a big trash bag.
there are tens of thousands of trash bins around Chicago, from the lake shore to the her parks. the best place to find a suitable trash bag is by the lake shore. every morning, the city puts fresh new trash bags in the bins, and since the tourists haven't arrived yet, there are much higher chances for finding a perfect trash bag. best type is an industrial size (55 gallon+) black trash bag. some transparent or white ones can be useful too. test the bag with your hands, try to tear it apart. if it gives you a nice strong resistance, it is the bag you are looking for.

Step #2: cut the bag open.
lie the bag flat in the shape of a rectangle, just like the original shape of this. find the side lines. cut the bag open into two pieces from there. (fig. 1)

Step #3: tie a weight on each of the four corners of the bag.
use some bricks, rocks or bottles. the best weight should be a little bit heavier than the bag itself. put the weight in the corner of the bag. tie it into the bag. (fig. 2)

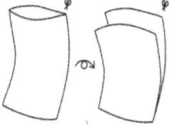

Step #4: a practice throw.
hold the bag as in stand to the side of the pigeon grup. throw the bag in a counter-clockwise direction (fig. 3,4). it might be a little bit rough on your first try, but you will catch up very quickly. Also, the bigger the pigeon group, the better chance you have.

Step #5: select two pigeons
a pigeon equals 1000 calories. the recommended calories an American should adult consume every day is 2000. two pigeons will be able to meet your daily need. set the rest free for the future.

KILL&GUT.

Step #1: smash the pigeon
there are several ways to kill the pigeon after you catch it. smashing it at the head will be the quickest way. the easiest way to smash the pigeon is to use the weight tied at the corner of your bag. give the pigeon a quick smash on the head. the bird is then ready to gut.

Step #2: find a knife
there are several materials around the city that can be used as a gutting knife (fig. 5).

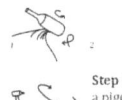

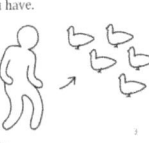

a glass bottle can be found easily around the following club districts (fig. 6). a razor fence can be found around the following factory areas (fig. 7). or, for more advanced skill levels you can make your own rock knife!

Step #3: find a working place
find a place with running water to gut your pigeon. the bathroom of a shopping mall, a grocery store or even a coffee shop can do the trick. because the gutting process can be a little bit bloody, a bathroom where you can lock your door will be ideal. the following places are the suggested working places (fig. 8)

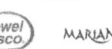

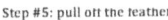

Step #5: pull off the feathers
there are two ways to get rid of the feathers. A. keep the hot water running, and it will be easy for you to pull off the feathers. B. cover the bird with mud. after cooking, the feathers will come off with the mud.

FIRE&COOK.

Step #1: find seasoning
salt and pepper can be found at restaurants with self-service bars. the following are some suggested places (fig. 10).

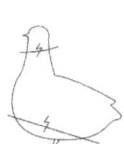

Step #2: build up a stove
there are hundreds of ways to build a stove. and since cooking will create a lot of smoke, finding a rural place to do it will be ideal. the following are far north and sounth beaches in Chicago that may be ideal for cooking. here is a suggested way to build a stove (fig. 11). the key is keep the air flow inside but not too much. a good outside stove needs to be short and small.

Step #3: set the fire.
gather newspapers and twigs for the fire. a lighter will be handy, but if you can't find a lighter, find a smoker.

Step #4: prepare your bird.
season your bird with pepper and salt inside out. cover your bird with sand. bury the bird inside the stove. follow the instruction. 20-30 min will be ideal for a pigeon to be cooked.

Step #4: gut your bird
cut the throat open and give a quick slide from the anus up to the chest (fig. 9). pull out all the guts inside and give the pigeon a nice wash.

TIPS. A. this introduction can be used to cook other birds.

B. some of the movement requires practice. but it is guaranteed for all ages and all body shapes.

C. there are some farmer's markets around Chicago. you can sell your cooked birds there. cooking the bird in front of people will be a nice traffic stop.

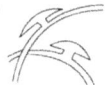

Vicky Yen

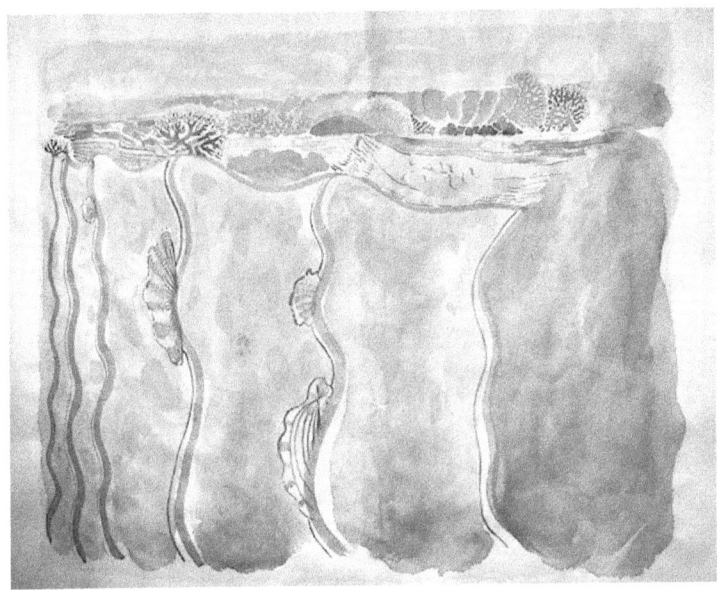

This is a drawing of an empty cliff underneath the ocean.

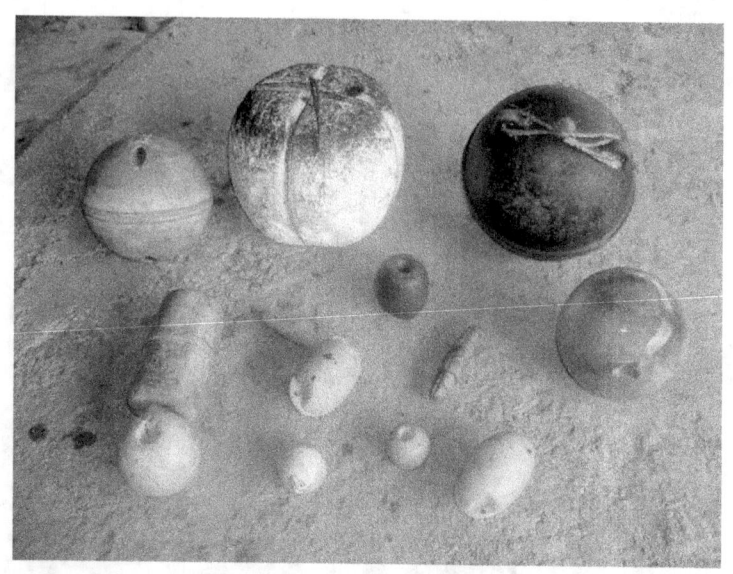

https://www.google.com/search?q=%E5%B
0%8F%E9%AD%9A%E6%B5%AE%E7%90%83&tbm=i
sch&ved=2ahUKEwjGkfePrKDoAhVVNaYKHUwj
DxEQ2-
cCegQIABAC&prmd=imnv&rlz=1CDGOYI_enTW
869TW869&safe=strict&hl=en-
US#imgrc=62WDhrZW2q0FGM&imgdii=tPCnpE
fTRykSrM

242

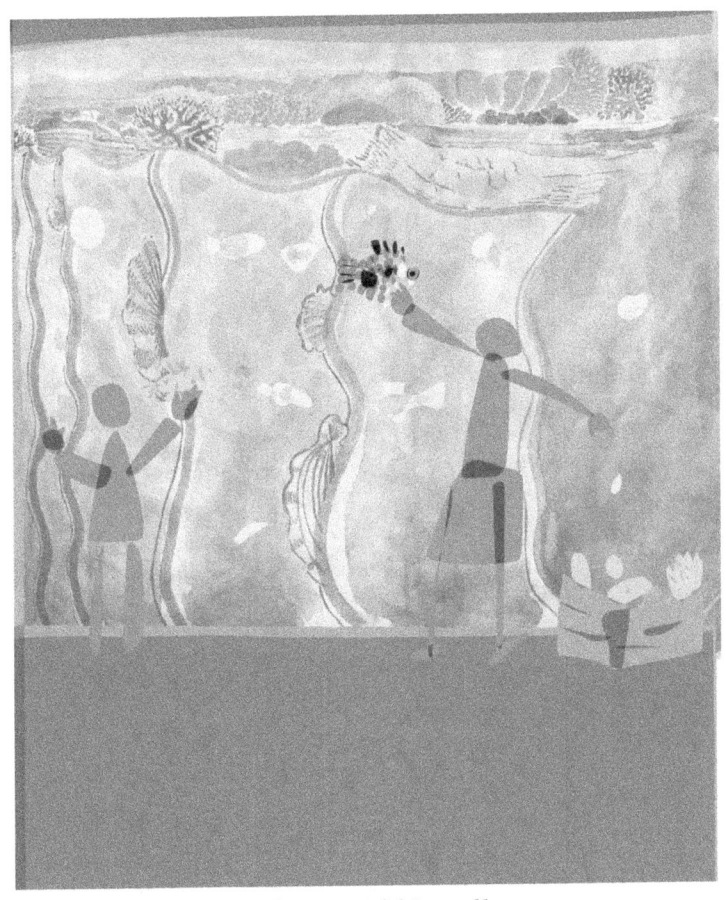

If this is a mural, and we could install ocean-waste art of the shapes of sea animals, corals, fish...

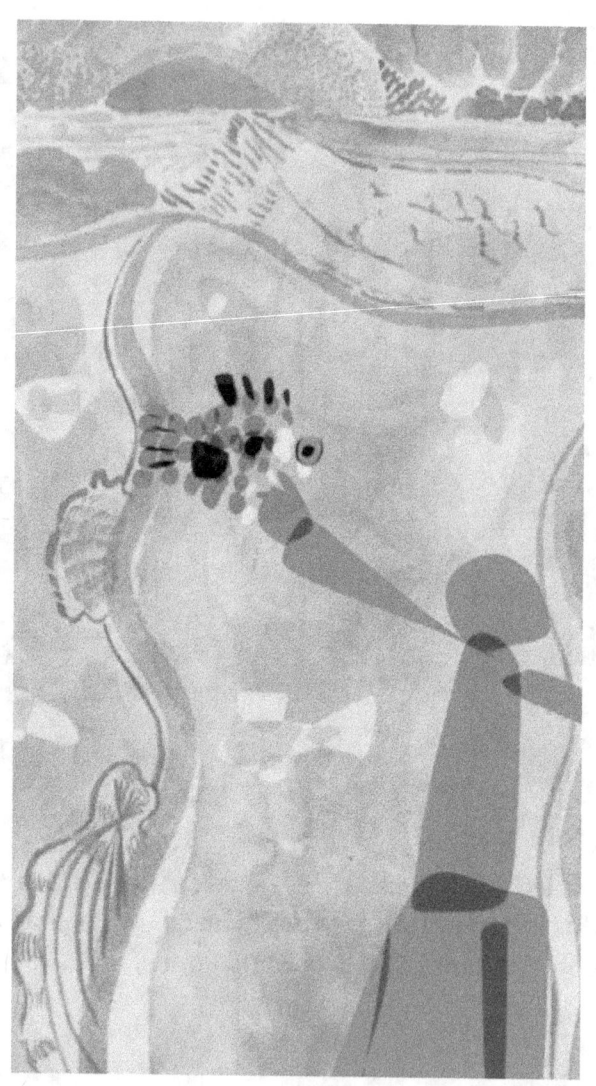

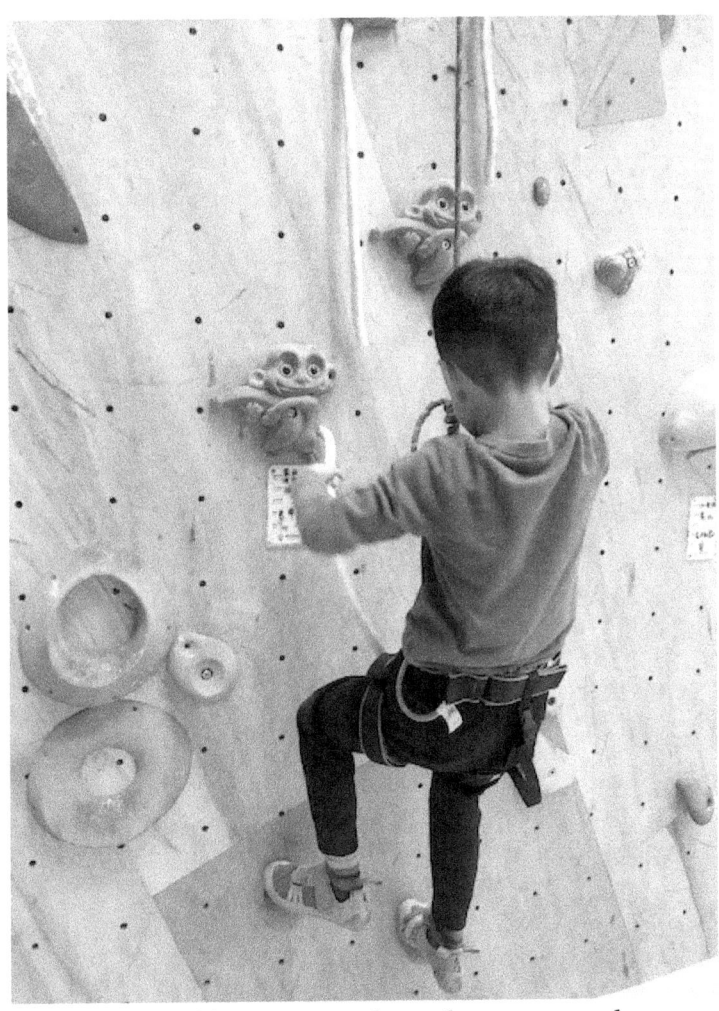

Students could learn more about the ocean, and perhaps, it could turn into a rock climbing wall!

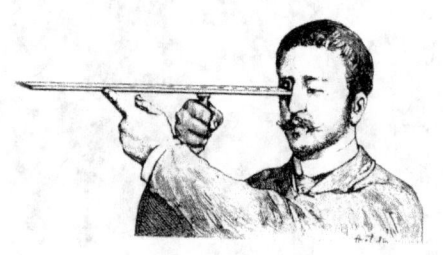

www.compoundyellow.com

2020